Working with Two-year-olds

Working with Two-year-olds is an accessible and practical guide into the developmental pathways of two-year-olds. The book uses established research and environmental and cultural effects to provide an essential background on two-year-old development, while incorporating reflective questions and tasks to encourage self-reflection throughout.

Divided into three clear parts, this book covers useful and interesting topics on the development of two-year-olds, such as:

- Emotional and social development
- Language and communicating
- Disposition and mindset
- Playful learning
- Family life
- Physical development

Providing theoretical overviews alongside practical ideas, and consistently encouraging critical self-reflection on all topics covered, Brierley has created an informative and constructive manual for students on Early Childhood courses and for practitioners and childminders on continuing professional development courses alike.

Julie Brierley is a lecturer in Education and programme director of PGCE Early Years (3-7 years) at the University of Hull, UK. Having 17 years' experience gained from working with two-year-old children, their families and nursery practitioners has inspired her to write this book.

Working with Two-year-olds
Developing Reflective Practice

Julie Brierley

LONDON AND NEW YORK

First published 2020
by Routledge
2 Park Square, Milton Park, Abingdon, Oxon, OX14 4RN

and by Routledge
52 Vanderbilt Avenue, New York, NY 10017

Routledge is an imprint of the Taylor & Francis Group, an informa business

© 2020 Julie Brierley

The right of Julie Brierley to be identified as author of this work has been asserted by her in accordance with sections 77 and 78 of the Copyright, Designs and Patents Act 1988.

All rights reserved. No part of this book may be reprinted or reproduced or utilised in any form or by any electronic, mechanical, or other means, now known or hereafter invented, including photocopying and recording, or in any information storage or retrieval system, without permission in writing from the publishers.

Trademark notice: Product or corporate names may be trademarks or registered trademarks, and are used only for identification and explanation without intent to infringe.

British Library Cataloguing-in-Publication Data
A catalogue record for this book is available from the British Library

Library of Congress Cataloging-in-Publication Data
A catalog record has been requested for this book

ISBN: 978-1-138-60062-1 (hbk)
ISBN: 978-1-138-60064-5 (pbk)
ISBN: 978-0-429-47081-3 (ebk)

Typeset in Optima
by Swales & Willis, Exeter, Devon, UK

To Joe, Hannah and Scott – all my love

Contents

About the author ix
Acknowledgements xi

Introduction 1

PART 1
Getting started with reflection **5**

1 The reflective practitioner 7
2 The foundations for learning: Developmental theory 21
3 Physical development: Moving to learn or learning to move? 33
4 Communication and language development: Competent communicators 45

PART 2
The building blocks for learning: The *how* of learning **57**

5 Family life 59
6 Dispositions and mindset 69
7 Key person 79

PART 3
The environment for learning: Provision and practice **95**

8 Playing and learning 97

Contents

9	Schema	109
10	The learning environment	123
11	The documentation process: Evidence of learning	137
	References	147
	Index	151

About the author

Julie Brierley is a lecturer at the University of Hull. She teaches on a range of early years courses. Julie originally qualified and worked as a primary teacher working mainly in Trafford Education Authority. After the birth of her own children, she moved to North Yorkshire and along with her husband took over the ownership and management of a private day nursery. It is from this her interest in two-year-old children developed. Julie's interest in young children's active movement and schema continued to grow as she studied for her MA and EdD at the University of Sheffield. Following the completion of her EdD Julie co-authored a book with Cathy Nutbrown titled *Understanding schematic learning at two*. The 17 years' of experience gained from working with two-year-old children, their families and nursery practitioners has formed the inspiration for this book.

Acknowledgements

The capabilities of two-year-old children only become visible as we spend time with them, becoming involved in their life and their experiences.

Julie expresses her sincere thanks to the parents, children and staff at the nursery for allowing her to get to know them and initiate her own journey of discovery. This book exists as a result of that journey.

Introduction

This book is a result of my journey of discovery, fuelled by my experience as a nursery manager and propelled by both professional and academic developments, the journey has lasted over two decades.

This book focuses specifically on two-year-olds, celebrating and understanding the joys and challenges; understanding and recognising two-year-old children have unique needs.

The second year of life is one of the most complex; developing independence, mastering spoken language, and controlling emotions are some of the overwhelming skills needing to be conquered at this early stage of life. Is it any wonder that two-year-old children feel frustrated as beneath the surface they are struggling to regulate their emotions, to develop control of their neural pathways while also trying to articulate a connection between abstract sounds and objects they desire?

It is intended that this book will provide knowledge tips and ideas to assist and underpin understanding of the uniqueness of being two. Writing this book, my aim has been for it to be read as if we were having a conversation, it is intended to be user friendly, but with enough theoretical content that keen readers will consider further study or move on to reading more theoretical texts.

The book aspires to support a reflective approach to knowledge development, encouraging a reflective approach to current understanding and assumptions around the needs of two-year-old children.

The initial chapter will introduce the concept of reflection and what it means to reflect on practice. Like any new skill 'reflection' requires practice, and determination if it is to become a natural and inherent habit within our daily practice with young children. The chapter will explore what it means to reflect critically. Alongside theoretical reflective frameworks, and examples of how reflection can be used to enhance knowledge and understanding around the needs of two-year-old children.

Introduction

The following three chapters will introduce **the foundations for learning – development theory**, a more in depth look at:

- Personal social and emotional development
- Physical development
- Communication and language development

While each aspect of development is discussed separately, the inherent message about the complexities and interconnectedness of young children development is stressed. The chapters provide opportunities to reflect upon held assumptions and knowledge of two-year-old children development.

Part two identifies **the building blocks for learning – the *how* of learning**. Chapter 5 considers the influencing and powerful role family culture and home learning exerts on young children's development. Chapter 6 identifies the importance of valuing the process of learning, how to develop positive dispositions and mindset through fostering the skills of resilience and perseverance. Chapter 7 reinforces two-year-olds need to feel safe and secure, emphasising the importance of developing an effective key person approach.

The environment for learning – provision and practice is discussed in Part three. Exploring and unpicking the characteristics of effective learning, Chapter 8 unravels what learning through play actually means. Providing guidance on the role of the adult in supporting two-year-old children's play.

Chapter 9 introduces the notion of schema. Knowledge of schema provides an opportunity to feed an inquisitive mind, to nourish curiosity, and extend a young child's thinking. Using schema as a basis from which to plan. Chapter 10 discovers how to organise and resource effective indoor and outdoor environments for two-year-old children. Chapter 11 takes an insightful look at the purpose and practice of recording two-year-old children's learning. Highlighting how reflecting on the observation process helps those who work and care for young children, to become informed and better able to support the learning and development process.

In this book the word

- *Nursery* refers to any setting two-year-old children may spend time.
- *Educator* refers to anyone working with young children.
- The words *young children* and *two-year-old* are used interchangeably.

How to use this book

This book requires a commitment and active engagement in the suggested activities. Each chapter includes questions and short sections to support the habit of reflective practice.

Key features in each chapter include:

Pause for thought

Reflective questions

Provides the chance to stop, to pause, to take time to consider ideas, views, beliefs and the opportunity to explore our assumptions.

Point of note
Point of action
Point of practice

While not requiring a specific action these highlighted information boxes provide vital information and ideas to consider.

Future Challenges

Each chapter closes with a challenge for the future.

Effective reflection takes practice, it comes from finding a process to suit the individual learner.

'Future Challenge' provides the opportunity to acquire the underpinning skills to facilitate the reflective habit.

PART 1
Getting started with reflection

# The reflective practitioner

While it may seem a bold statement to make, it is essential to acknowledge that reflecting on practice is critical when working with two-year-old children. In an ever-changing world, it is vital that early years practitioners continue to further their skills and knowledge to meet the needs of the children and families they work alongside.

Without reflection, it will be difficult, if not impossible to define and refine practice to ensure suitable responses to meet the individual needs of every child. Reflection forms a crucial role in our practice with two-year-old children. The ability to enhance practice with young children and respond to new initiatives has become a daily expectation of all who work with young children in the 21st century.

Reading about theory and child development is essential for developing knowledge, but done in isolation, it can be a mechanical approach to knowledge development. The process of reflection requires the ability to think critically and creatively, to construct and share a personal interpretation in response to a particular context or occurrence.

Findings from my own experience show how the use of reflection empowers individuals to make informed decisions with regards to their daily practice with young children. The process of reflection ensures we consider other options and ideas; to develop a greater understanding of particular situations.

Reflection can be used to look back on past situations, to ask questions, to ponder and wonder why.

> An individual does not stop learning and developing once they have completed their initial training and become qualified … they need further training to enhance and develop their knowledge and skills, and to keep pace with new research and developments.
>
> (Nutbrown 2012: 50)

Getting started with reflection

Reflection has the potential to make a difference, supporting an ongoing learning journey for individuals alongside the opportunity for professional development. The challenge we face; *how* reflection can be embedded into everyday practice with those who work with two-year-old children, *how* to develop reflective habits.

> **Pause for thought**
>
> What are my beliefs about reflection?
>
> How will it feel to reflect?
>
> Why is reflection relevant to me, and my work with two-year-olds?

Participating in the reflective activities provided within this book will help to develop a reflective attitude and habit. Providing the reader with an opportunity to critically consider and question the beliefs, ideas and practices they follow when working alongside and supporting two-year-old children.

If you are looking for a book, that merely requires you to be a passive reader, this is not the book for you. This book requires a commitment and active engagement in the suggested activities.

The reflective journey

Exploring what it means to be reflective and introducing the concept of critical reflection, the chapter will illustrate how cultivating the habit of reflection results in better understanding. The knowledge and confidence required for supporting two-year-old children and their families increases.

Starting the reflective journey is not a difficult task; it does, however, require active participation. If we consider reflection as a substitute for our thought process, we can look back at events and start to ask questions.

Reflective questions help to identify what we already know and consider how we might want to improve or refine a situation. The words what, why, how, can, where, when and who are essential in forming reflective questions.

> **Pause for thought**
>
> Reflect on your time at work today.
>
> What were you most proud of?
>
> Where did you encounter struggle today?
>
> How did you deal with it?

Reflecting on an event or situation provides the opportunity for more in-depth learning, evoking new ways of working. It is, however, essential to recognise that to reflect, means more than to think back to a situation. To reflect we have to be honest to self-assess our practice and competence (knowledge) at that given time.

Reflecting is an active and dynamic process; it is about taking ownership of the thinking process, looking for learning points, striving for a better understanding. To do this, we must be honest about our knowledge and understanding, and most importantly we must want to do it!

Reflection involves challenging and developing existing knowledge. In striving for a greater understanding, we begin to recognise our own capabilities, knowledge and values. Without reflection, we will continue to repeat and do the same thing again and again. There is a real possibility our practice will merely stagnate.

> **Point of note**
>
> Reflection is the key to reviewing and evaluating practice, it enables practitioners to question, agree, disagree and challenge practice and provision.

Looking for answers and possibilities

Formal reflection requires us to look further than our own assumptions and beliefs. It requires us to draw not only on our inbuilt understanding but also on current research, theory and practice. **Formal reflection** places us, the learner, in the powerful position of being able to seek new knowledge, ideas and understanding. **Formal reflection** provides the opportunity to further our learning, to ensure our practice meets the needs of today's two-year-old children and their families. Importantly it becomes a process for continuing towards our professional development.

Perhaps some of the misconceptions and misunderstandings around reflection are due to the complexity of language and terminology that unfold as we start to explore the key ideas and definitions of reflection.

The following definitions provide an initial starting point for understanding the different reflective vocabulary:

Reflection: Is 'an important human activity in which people recapture their experience, think about it, mull it over and evaluate it' (Boud, Keogh and Walker 1985: 43). Put simply reflection is the processing of knowledge (Moon 2004).

Informal reflection: Draws on self-questioning; it develops an awareness of our assumptions. It sanctions the use of questioning to establish why we do what we do.

Formal reflection: Engaging with current theory and research promotes greater understanding and knowledge, empowering the possibility to think critically and creatively to construct a new and deeper understanding.

Reflective writing: Uses writing as a way to extend the thought process.

Critical reflection: Critically reflective practitioners can communicate and share the rationale behind their practice, explain why they do what they do! Knowing why we believe what we believe, happens when we question our assumptions and practices through the process of critical reflection.

Reflective practice/practitioner: The ongoing habit of critically reflecting on everyday practice and occurrences.

The following observation illustrates a snapshot view of a typical episode in the day of a two-year-old. The observation is followed by a reflective discussion to illustrate how reflection can be used as a tool to enhance knowledge and understand two-year-old children's thinking and behaviour.

The reflective practitioner

> **Observation**
>
> *Tilly loved jigsaw puzzles; she would spend vast amounts of time completing jigsaw puzzles both at home and nursery. Tilly's key worker suspected her interests in these puzzles demonstrated aspects of a containing schema.*
>
> *Today Tilly was engaged with her favourite jigsaw, she placed the pieces in the correct place, seemingly with ease. She smiled as she placed the last piece. Her attention then turned to the shape puzzle. She emptied all the pieces from the frame and set about replacing the parts. The triangle shape seemed to be causing her an issue, she attempted to turn the shape, but still, it did not fit into the space.*
>
> *Tilly pushed the puzzle from the table to the floor. The shape pieces bounced in all directions across the floor. Tilly walked away … when asked to come and help pick up the pieces Tilly was very reluctant.*

Reflecting on Tilly's play episode provides an opportunity to make sense of the situation, to formulate ideas.

We can mull this event over in our minds, take some time to think about it and devise an understanding of the incident. Reflecting on the episode provides the opportunity to recognise and question our assumptions and beliefs about two-year-old children and their expected behaviour.

If we accept actions based on our assumptions we may believe Tilly was behaving, as we would expect a two-year-old to behave.

If we adopt a more **formal reflective** stance the process of **critically reflecting** allows us to pose questions as to why Tilly responded in this way. Tilly is usually a reasonably calm child, throwing the jigsaw to the floor is not one of her typical responses to a situation.

Searching beyond our innate knowledge, engaging with child development theory promotes greater understanding and knowledge, empowering the possibility to think critically and creatively to construct a new and deeper understanding. Providing the opportunity to pose a more creative interpretation of the incident.

It is possible that in struggling with the puzzle piece, Tilly became frustrated with the puzzle. This episode did not 'fit' with her previous learning experiences, in the past when Tilly experienced difficulty she found jiggling the jigsaw pieces allowed them to slot into place.

A suggested interpretation may be Tilly was experiencing 'cognitive discomfort'; this is possibly the first time she had experienced this emotion. Finding out more about Tilly's schematic behaviour could provide the opportunity to gain a greater understanding of her cognitive development (Brierley and Nutbrow 2018), while

Getting started with reflection

also offering guidance on how best to respond and enhance the provision offered to Tilly.

The use of **formal reflection** provided a plan with a route to deeper learning and understanding of Tilly's behaviour. The **critical reflection** process can develop the underpinning skills to facilitate learning from practice, to help us understand why Tilly may have behaved in this way. Engaging with formal and critical reflective processes provides us with new learning opportunities and increased confidence in our ability to support Tilly.

The opportunity to increase our knowledge and understanding also facilitates the possibility of further supporting Tilly. Through our new and increased understanding of schema theory, we can develop the provision to provide new play experiences to extend Tilly's schematic learning experiences and further develop her understanding and learning.

Further information around schema and how to enhance provision for two-year-old children is explored in Chapters 8 and 9.

> **Pause for thought**
>
> Considering your day at work, what assumptions have you made today, with regards to children's behaviour?
>
> What assumptions do you hold about two-year-old children's behaviour?

Choosing which incidents to reflect upon can be difficult; often the incidents that remain in our minds are those episodes that did not go well or stand out for some reason.

However, it is also vital to reflect on good practice, things you feel you do well. This provides the opportunity to consider why they are successful and how to replicate them in the future – to develop our practice.

> **Point of note**
>
> The ability to recognise effective practice is essential if it is to be replicated and used in situations that you may find more challenging.

The nature of reflection

The initial concepts of reflection come from the work of Dewey (1938) who recognised three important characteristics essential to the reflective practitioner; *open-mindedness* to new ideas; *wholeheartedness* to search and accept new ideas, and *responsibility* to understand and accept the consequences of your actions.

Dewey's concepts highlight *routine actions* as merely going through the motions, suggesting those who follow routines without questioning can become static and unresponsive to the needs of individual children.

In contrast, Dewey describes 'reflective action' that evolves through the process of self-appraisal and self-development, the willingness to learn and develop. It is imperative those working alongside young children must always be thinking about what they are doing, considering their responses and actions.

> **Pause for thought**
>
> Consider your time at work today.
>
> What did you learn today?
>
> How did this learning come about?
>
> What will you do differently tomorrow?

Responding to young children in the moment is vital. Thinking on your feet, making a conscious decision to change or adapt the practice to support an individual's need or new situations is an essential aspect of effective practice with two-year-old children.

No matter how much organising and planning is undertaken prior to a situation it is vital we continue to make ongoing in the moment judgements and decisions about how we respond to two-year-old children and individual circumstances.

Getting started with reflection

Schon (1983) describes such spontaneity as ***reflection-in-action***. Alternatively looking back after the session, or after an event has happened is described by Schon (1983) as ***reflection-on-action***.

Reflection-on-action is looking back, it can only be done retrospectively, once the situation has happened and a possible solution has been found. This then involves asking questions such as:

- *Was this the right solutions?*
- *Were there other solutions?*
- *What would/could have been the consequences if different solutions had been found? – If only I had ...*

The reflective practitioner must aim to develop actions that emerge through professional thinking. Therefore, it is crucial also to think ahead and consider what might happen, how might a two-year-old child respond to a particular situation? The process of looking forward is considered by Pollard (2014) as ***reflection-before-action***.

Reflection-before-action is about thinking things through beforehand, possibly coming up with an alternative or better solution. *If I do it this way, I think this may happen.*

Pause for thought

Consider your last day at work, can you think of an occasion when you have used:

- Reflection-in-action
- Reflection-on-action
- Reflection-before-action

What type of reflection feels most comfortable? Why do you think this might be?

What type of reflection feels more difficult? Why do you think this might be?

Reflective practice is a cyclic and dynamic process intended to scaffold and develop effective practice. Evolving through the continuous requirement to *monitor, evaluate* and *revise* our actions and responses.

There is a myriad of models and frameworks, to describe, guide and scaffold the reflective process. However, it is crucial reflective processes are not used simply as recipes, or instructions to be slavishly followed.

Reflecting must not become a mechanical process; it needs to be valued as an opportunity to draw upon and engage with our own professional judgments, feelings and values. The learning process is dynamic and varies for each and every individual. Effective reflection comes from finding a process to suit the individual learner, the ability to acquire the underpinning skills to facilitate reflective learning, to gain the habit of reflection.

Reflective practice is a process we adopt to help gain a deeper understanding of our *practice*; the ability to communicate and share the rationale behind our practice. What is relevant; is we learn from our reflection.

Point of note

Being a reflective practitioner helps us to increase our skills, understanding and learning. It results in our being more effective practitioners (Macleod-Brunell 2004: 45).

Reflective writing is an established technique to facilitate reflective practice. Reflective writing provides an opportunity to make sense of our experiences; Moon (2004a) advocates the use of diaries, learning logs/journals, portfolios or narratives to write down experiences as a way of aiding and scaffolding the reflection process.

Writing provides the time to stop and think, to engage in constructing a personal interpretation in response to a particular experience or occurrence.

Using diaries, learning logs/journals, portfolios to write down experiences provide a way of aiding reflection. Journal writing offers an opportunity to make sense of experience through the use of a written explanation. Writing provides personal independence, it requires us to stop and think forcing us, to question and explore ideas and concepts, to find a solution or justify an action.

Reflective writing

Reflective journal:

- Your reaction to the event
- Different ways you might look at it
- How the experience links with others

- How you can understand the experience in the light of a theory
- What you have learnt
- What you need to learn
- How you might achieve your learning

A narrative is a story of an experience:

- Written in the first person
- Learner-centred in that it allows the learner's voice to be heard
- Enables links to be made between personal and professional development

Enables us to:

- Be conscious of our potential for bias and discrimination
- Make the best use of the knowledge available
- Challenge and develop the existing professional knowledge base
- Avoid past mistakes
- Maximise our opportunities for learning

Group reflection

An individual's knowledge can limit reflective learning, true reflective depth will take time and practice and needs to be enriched with opportunities to engage with peers.

Sharing experiences with peers enables differing thoughts and ideas to be considered, the exchange of views between colleagues and parents presents a further opportunity for knowledge and understanding to develop. Opportunities for group discussion and reflection are a powerful and vital tool in developing and progressing practice with two-year-old children and their families.

Theoretical models of reflection

Theoretical reflective models provide a structure to guide and scaffold the reflective process helping to deconstruct experiences to access deeper level reflections. The most well-known reflective cycles are Kolb (1984) experiential cycle and Gibbs

(1988) reflective cycle. Used effectively these models enable us to formulate new thinking that can then be used and tested in our future practice.

Kolb (1984) experiential cycle and Gibbs (1988) reflective cycle models can be used initially to promote reflective thoughts within the mind and then to create written forms to help represent and solidify abstract ideas and thoughts.

Kolb's experiential learning cycle (1984)

Believing any experience has the potential to support learning, Kolb (1984) identifies a cycle of four stages that have to be considered, and reflected on, in order to recognise potential learning.

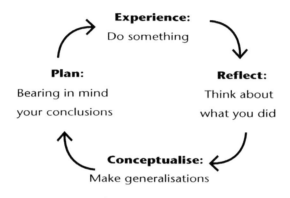

Figure 1.1 Kolb's experiential learning cycle

Stage 1 Experience: Select the experience to reflect upon
Stage 2 Reflect: Reflect on the experience

- *What happened?*
- *What was my role in the experience?*

Stage 3 Conceptualise: Interpreting the event making suggestions or a hypothesis about the experience

- *This is what I did, why do I do it like this?*
- *Are there other solutions, maybe better solutions? – New knowledge.*

Getting started with reflection

Stage 4 Plan: In this stage, we try the new solutions

- *Try out what you have learnt.*

Kolb's cycle provides the opportunity to recognise and reflect on experiences to incorporate new knowledge and ideas and then to try out what you have learnt.

Gibbs' six stages reflective cycle (1988)

Expanding on Kolb's ideas, Gibbs' reflective cycle (1988) has six steps to consider and work through. Recognising links between theory and practice, the cycle challenges self-held assumptions, empowering individuals to move from simply describing what happened to analyse and developing future action. Exploring new ideas to try and find alternative approaches and solutions aims to prompt self-improvement and stimulate changes to practice.

Emotions can play a huge role when working with two-year-old children and their families. Acknowledging and accepting the role emotion plays in our work is vital to improving practice with two-year-old children and their families.

The success of Gibbs' reflective cycle (1988) to bring about change in attitude and practices, may well be down to the recognition of the role of emotion.

Figure 1.2 Gibbs' reflective cycle

1. **Description**: What happened?

    - *Provide a concise description of the experience*

2. **Feelings**: This is a descriptive account of your thinking and feeling. The recognition of the role emotion can play in a situation.

    - *How did you feel prior to the experience?*
    - *How did you feel and what were you thinking during the experience?*
    - *How did you react during the experience?*
    - *How did you feel and what did you think after the experience?*

3. **Evaluation**: This involves making judgements about the experience? Challenging assumptions.

    - *What went well during the experience?*
    - *What went poorly during the experience?*
    - *How did the experience finish?*
    - *Was there a resolution or was it left incomplete?*

4. **Analysis**: This part is analytical, trying to explain the causes and consequences, to ask questions like why? So what? Moreover, what if? What sense can you make of the situation? Your theoretical knowledge today.

    - *Reconsider what went well – why do you think they went well?*
    - *Reconsider what went poorly – what are the consequences of this action?*
    - *Consider how decisive action could have been further improved?*
    - *Think about your contribution to the experience – how useful was it and why?*
    - *Did a previous experience help you?*

5. **Conclusion**: What have you learnt from the experience?

    - *What should or could I have done differently?*
    - *What stopped me doing this?*
    - *What did I learn about my current knowledge and practice?*

6. **Action plan**: What actions do you need to take to improve and increase your knowledge? Empowering changes to practice.

    - *How can I be better prepared for next time?*

- *How can I further improve the outcome?*
- *What areas/aspects do I need to develop further?*
- *What specific steps do I need to take to achieve these improvements?*

Reflection is a highly skilled activity requiring practice, it does not always come naturally; you will need to work hard to build and establish your reflective habit. It is essential to find a reflective model or framework that best fits your individual needs. In time it may be you who creates your own model to suit your personal reflective thinking style.

As you move through the book, you will be asked and encouraged to develop your reflective habit. Each chapter provides occasions to *pause for thought*, the chance and opportunity to question and mull over your thoughts around a specific topic or aspect of your practice.

The close of each chapter encourages engagement with a theoretical model of reflection, providing the opportunity to scaffold and guide reflective thoughts. This final reflection encourages group reflection, a process of sharing and developing discussion with colleagues.

Experience advocates, the use of diaries, learning logs/journals, portfolios or narratives to record your reflective experiences. Returning to these thoughts provides a way of aiding and scaffolding a more in-depth reflective process, and a record of your reflective journey.

Involvement in these activities will improve your reflective habit alongside developing knowledge and understanding two-year-old children and their families: used appropriately these activities can support your professional development.

The foundations for learning

Developmental theory

Personal, social and emotional development

Attention to young children's personal social and emotional development has to be a priority, bathed in an environment of love recognition and support two-year-old children will grow into resilient and self-assured adults.

Addressing the social and emotional needs of two-year-olds will make a difference in their whole lives. Educators and parents are in the privileged position of helping to shape these new young lives. This chapter will provide an overview of the theoretical framework surrounding young children's personal, social and emotional development. The chapter includes opportunities to reflect upon the beliefs and knowledge you hold around the personal, social and emotional development of two-year-old children.

The following chapters will pose questions to the reader encourage a *pause for thought*, personal reflective moments, these aim not just to support individual understanding and learning, but also to help develop the confidence to share and discuss ideas with others.

Getting started

The importance of attachment cannot be underestimated. Attachments are the relationships all young children build with the special people in their lives. Attachment theory illustrates how baby's and young children look to particular people for security, comfort and protection.

Getting started with reflection

> **Pause for thought**
>
> Attachment theory.
>
> What is your understanding of attachment theory?
>
> How does attachment theory influence your daily practice with two-year-olds?

Attachment

The emotional bonds two-year-old children develop with their parents, and other caregivers are crucial for their personal, social and emotional development. A young child with a secure attachment feels able to rely on their parents or caregivers for safety and comfort. Two-year-old children use these meaningful attachment relationships as bases from which to explore the world.

Bowlby's (1988) research into attachment illustrates how secure attachment plays an essential role in the survival of babies and young children. In stressful or frightening situations secure attachments ensure young children to seek protection from his/her attached figure.

Bowlby (1988) also highlighted the importance of attachment stating the quality of attachment formed has a significant factor on a child's future development, stimulating either a self-confident and emotionally stable personality with great capacities for learning or an individual with social-emotional, behavioural, and/or cognitive problems.

Attachment relationships form through a cyclic process, the child signals, caregivers respond to the signal eliciting a positive response from the child. One of the main conditions for ensuring the development of secure attachment requires babies and young children receiving timely and appropriate responses to their signals (Ainsworth et al. 1978). Meaning that successful attachment depends on the parent or carer responding to the child's signals in such a way that the child feels loved, nurtured and safe. As the cycle of signal and successful response continues, the attachment relationship develops.

The ability to recognise, interpret and respond correctly to a young child's signal requires adults who are sensitive and emotionally available. Babies and young children will only form attachments with those who respond appropriately to their signals.

The foundations for learning

> **Points for practice**
>
> Attachment theory is often associated with babies and very young children. However, the implications of attachment theory can apply to any point throughout a young person's life.

More importantly, when forming attachments, the quality of the interactions between the child and the adult has a greater significance to the developing relationship than the actual time spent together. Suggesting that attachments develop as a result of the *quality of interactions* and communication shared between the young child and adult.

Young children are capable of forming multiple attachments: all adults responding with a sensitive, appropriate and timely reply to the child's signals will succeed in building an attachment. However, usually the attachment children form with parents will be more intense, explaining why it is the parent they will seek and return to if they require reassurance.

> **Pause for thought**
>
> Consider the children you work with.
>
> What signals do they make?
>
> How do you respond?
>
> What can you do to build attachment relationships with children in your care?

Within a nursery setting, it is crucial the key worker becomes the special person who understands and provides a secure base for the child. Two-year-old children need the opportunity to develop trusting relationships within the nursery environment. Forming a secure attachment to a key person who will always respond appropriately to their signals and needs. The key person role will be further explored in Chapter 7.

> **Points for practice**
>
> Babies and young children build attachments as a result of adults responding to and meeting their emotional needs.
>
> The key emotional needs of all human beings are considered as:
>
> | | |
> |---|---|
> | Attention | Respect |
> | Acceptance | Support |
> | Appreciation | Comfort |
> | Encouragement | Approval |
> | Affection | Security |

Attachment theory has been well documented over the years. Research around attachment theory suggests the securely attached child develops a sense of worth and self-confidence, increased social skills, advanced cognitive abilities and better self-regulating capacities. In contrast, a child with an insecure attachment lacks confidence and has little sense of worth.

Attachment theory is often associated with young children and babies. Those who work with two-year-olds in nurseries must also recognise and understand the ongoing implications of attachment theory. Two-year-old children have specific attachment needs that *must* be met.

Attachment behaviours

Some two-year-olds will not yet have built up enough emotional resilience to deal with many of the situations they encounter during their day. It is important to recognise and understand the behaviour displayed at times by two-year-old children is quite normal for the stage of their development.

> **Pause for thought**
>
> Two-year-olds and behaviour.
>
> Is there behaviour displayed by young children that particularly bothers you?
>
> What could be the possible psychological meaning of the behaviours?

The foundations for learning

Two-year-old children will often have a need to feel physically close or maintain visual sight with their safe base, their key person, they may wish to stay within close proximity of the person to whom they have an attachment.

Points for practice

Setting that has a free flow play policy can be daunting for some two-year-olds, who wish to stay within close proximity to their special person.
Identify children who stay close to their familiar person during free play activities.
Recognise if children can make independent play choices.
Note children who can become unsettled during free play activities or tidy up time.

It may be they are happy to maintain a visual sighting only, or it may be that they continually return to touch base as it were, to gain additional reassurance. Some children will need to seek physical contact, wanting their key person to cuddle or pick them up, seemingly only a moment later they want to be free again.

Two-year-old children are likely to be very wary of unfamiliar adults.

When approached by an unfamiliar adult, young children will move close to their parents or familiar person to seek reassurance, children will often be asked to be picked up, or move behind adults' legs as if hiding. As young children gain more experience of seeing and meeting new people such behaviours will dissipate.

Points for practice

The anxiety two-year-old children display when meeting new people has enormous implications for starting at nursery. The settling in process and the daily transitions need to be purposefully planned.

Children who have secure attachments **will** demonstrate distress and separation anxiety if they find themselves in a situation without any of the people to whom they have an attachment. Two-year-old children will shout and scream in an attempt to signal that they need help. This is normal behaviour and can last for an extended period, such behaviour will not just disappear. These situations need to be considered and planned for.

Getting started with reflection

> **Pause for thought**
>
> Consider how you protect children against separation anxiety, during the settling in process?

In 2010 National Strategies published a selection of guidance documents to support practitioners working in the early year's foundation stage.

The following activity can be completed individually or as a team activity. The activity aims to develop discussion and sharing of ideas and understanding around the attachment needs of two-year-old children.

Think about the evidence of Maisy's attachment in the following example.

Mel and Maisy have been shopping. On the way home, they stop at Mel's mother's house. They often do this because it is quite a long walk back home and Maisy who is 26 months loves to see her Grandma. She is tired when they arrive and, when a man she does not know opens the door, Maisy bursts into tears and clings to her Mum's legs. Mel lifts her up, cuddles her and tells her Grandma is coming. Grandma smiles and introduces Tom who is laying a new carpet in the hall. They leave Tom in the hall and go into the kitchen. Maisy lets Mel put her down, and she gives her Grandma her usual kiss and cuddle but keeps looking through into the hall. Grandma asks Tom if he would like another cup of tea. They both laugh when he says, no, thanks, he's had three already. Maisy has a drink and then stands and watches Tom. When he speaks to her, she looks back to her Mum for reassurance. Mum smiles and talks with Tom herself. Eventually, Tom and Maisy are having a conversation, and Maisy is 'helping' Tom but every now and then she turns around for reassurance, looking first at Mel and then at Grandma.

Reflect and note:
How Mel and her mother reassure Maisy.
How Maisy knows she can rely on them.
How they help her to become confident with Tom.

Her mother and grandmother are taking their lead from Maisy. They understand that it is healthy for a young child to be wary of people she doesn't know. They let Maisy take her time to feel comfortable.

Consider the implications for your practice?

- Managing staff shifts
- Holiday cover
- Room transitions
- New starters

Taken from DCSF (2010) *Social and Emotional Aspects of Development: Guidance for Practitioners Working in the Early Years Foundation Stage* Nottingham: DCSF Publications.

Two-year-old children who become withdrawn, quiet and passive can also be displaying signals of separation anxiety. Separation anxiety can be avoided when children and parents are given the opportunity to build relationships and make attachments with key workers and setting staff. The role of the key person will be further explored in Chapter 7.

Points for practice

Hints and tips for settling new children into the nursery

Use home and setting visits to build communication and relationships with families.

Allow children to remain with the same caregiver for an extended period of time.

Consider the child's cultural diversity.

Find out about the child's preferences and home routine.

Have family photographs on display in the setting.

Establish good-bye rituals, to help ease separation anxiety each day.

Ensure stability of personnel working in the nursery room.

Circumstances affecting attachment

Initial attachments are formed as parents spend time smiling, cooing, cuddling, touching and soothing their babies. Unfortunately, some factors can prevent parents from being emotionally available to display the required attachment responses.

- Mental health issues are becoming more common; the NHS (2019) report 1 in 10 women experience a form of depression after childbirth.
- Parents who have drug or alcohol issues may demonstrate inconsistency with their responses.
- The attachment cycle can be challenging to initiate with babies born prematurely due to the medical intervention required.

Research also suggests that parents who themselves experienced difficult childhoods, can find it harder to establish and maintain the attachment cycle.

Children who seem secure and thriving can also be affected by circumstances that are beyond their control;

- Parent in hospital
- Moving home
- Bereavement in the family
- Changes in daily routines
- A parent working away from home
- Parents separating
- Parent has a new partner
- A new baby in the family
- Drug or alcohol misuse

Changes in a two-year-old child's home life are often displayed through a change in behaviour in the nursery. It is important to be alert to such situations, two-year-old children will demonstrate more significant needs and parents may also need additional advice.

Self-esteem and confidence

Attachments provide children with the security that they are safe and cared for, and those who look after them are reliable. With this knowledge comes the confidence to explore the world more independently.

Self-confidence is linked to the quality of relationships young children have with adults. Meaning two-year-old children's confidence levels can vary across different environments. At home, a child can be considered confident by parents, but in a setting appear to lack confidence.

> **Pause for thought**
>
> Self-esteem and confidence.
>
> What does a confident two-year-old look like?
>
> Can a quiet child be confident?
>
> Observe if different environments affect children's confidence levels?

Self-confidence is closely linked to self-esteem, and what we feel about ourselves. Between 18-24 months young children can recognise themselves in a mirror or a photograph, from two-years onwards gender identification begins. Initially distinguishing if they are a boy or a girl, and identifying gender in other children.

Throughout childhood self-esteem and self-confidence continues to develop, during this time the caregiver's role is very influential in ensuring children maintain a positive self-image of themselves. From the age of two-years, children start to make judgements, to self-evaluate and form opinions about themselves.

For further information see Chapter 5 family life-home learning environment and Chapter 6 dispositions and growth mindset.

The development of friendship

Most research implies two-year-old children are self-absorbed and egocentric, meaning it is unrealistic to expect a two-year-old to share, take turns or form friendships. However, recent research into young children's schema suggests two-year-old children who share a schematic interest are capable of co-operation and over time a closeness, very much akin to friendship.

Observing and paying attention to other children's play exploits builds young children's confidence. Consistency of environment and peer group, alongside sensitive and responsive adults allows two-year-olds to recognise others with similar play interests. While their 'friendship' is initiated by mutual play interests, the closeness and attachment these children display for each other are evident.

The concept of schema is explored in depth in Chapter 9.

Getting started with reflection

> **Pause for thought**
>
> Consider your key children's play.
>
> What does friendship look like when you are two-years-old?
>
> Which children have similar play interests?

Emotional control

During the first few years of life, children's behaviour is mainly controlled through emotional impulses, through their fight and flight responses. The frontal lobes of the brain being responsible for cognitive functions and control of movement are not yet developed. Meaning two-year-old children have very little control over their reactions and actions when put under pressure.

> **Points for practice**
>
> Brain fact; what is sometimes known as the reptilian part of the brain controls our basic survival responses, our response to the threat. In situations where we feel threatened, unsafe or insecure our natural reaction will be either; fright – we freeze and become unresponsive, flight – running away or fight – we display an aggressive response. During this time rational thinking is not a possibility.

Two-year-olds can be very impulsive, and frequently appear to lack self-control. If they see something they want, their impulse will be to take it, they are not yet able to process and consider the consequences of their actions. This may result in such impulsive behaviour as pushing other children out of their way or snatching equipment.

> **Points for practice**
>
> **Safety point**
> Young children's inability to control their behaviour has enormous implications for their physical safety.

Reasoning and recapping a situation with a two-year-old is pointless, a two-year-old will not be able to tell you why they did it! Through gradual brain maturation processes, young children's self-control will develop, but initially, it can fluctuate causing two-year-old children's responses to be inconsistent. A two-year-old may be able to avoid temptation in the morning, but later in the day demonstrate less self-control.

Many two-year-old children know what not to do, but cannot always not do it. Manning-Morton and Thorpe (2015) compare it to the will power required by adults to stop smoking or successfully complete a diet.

Two-year-old children quickly become frustrated as they struggle to manage their impulsivity; such behaviour is often described as a tantrum. Dealing with two-year-olds behaviour requires the need to demonstrate patience and recognition and consideration of possible triggers. Tiredness and hunger can be significant factors in a two-year-old child's attempt to regulate emotions.

Points for practice

- Consider sleep and nap times that are appropriate.
- Greater flexibility around meal and snack times may be needed for two-year-old children.

Tantrums diminish as young children's language skills develop. The ability to communicate and express wishes alongside understanding simple explanations, 'wash hands then snack time', reduces the levels of frustration experienced by the child.

It is important not to become complacent and simply consider tantrums as part of life when working with two-year-olds. Dealing with frequent tantrums can be difficult, in such situations it is not uncommon to consider if the outburst is due to frustration or a learnt response that enables the young child to get what they want. It is important to adopt a consistent approach, especially if a child is displaying a learnt response.

Regardless, tantrums are distressing experiences for children and prevention is always a better option. Partnership with parents is vital to ensure two-year-old children do not receive mixed messages. Working and developing partnerships with parents is the focus of Chapter 5.

While it is not always possible to give a young child what they want, providing options and choices allows a two-year-old to maintain some power over the situation. Remember some age-related impulsiveness can be predicted, plan ahead (reflection–before action) by removing things that may cause frustration and lead to tantrums.

Future challenge

Take some time to consider and reflect how you *Support young children's personal, social and emotional development.*

Take some time to review and reflect on how:

- The daily routines
- The physical environment
- The key person role

can influence two-year-old children's behaviour.

Using a reflective model to guide your reflection. The following prompts illustrate how Gibbs reflective cycle supports and scaffolds the process of reflection.

1. Observe a child for a day, identify if/how behaviour changes at different points of the day. Record the observation using either written or photographic methods.
2. Acknowledge your feelings, how did the child's behaviour make you feel?
3. How does the physical and psychological environment impact on the child's personal, social and emotional development? How is this demonstrated?
4. What does this mean for the child's personal, social and emotional development? How could these experiences be improved?
5. What have you learnt about yourself from this experience? What have you discovered about the child you observed?
6. Going forward, how can you reinforce opportunities for personal, social and emotional development in the daily routine?

What have *you* gained from this reflection? Share your thoughts and ideas with colleagues.

Physical development
Moving to learn or learning to move?

Physical development plays a central role in young children's development. Unfortunately, in today's society, a continual focus on intellectual and cognitive skills repeatedly means the importance of physical development is overlooked in terms of its importance in the education spectrum. It would appear that life in the 21st century seems to neglect the importance and necessity of two-year-old children's need for physical movement.

The significance of physical development means it should not be underestimated or simply left to chance, its interconnectedness is far-reaching, forming the foundations from which *all* future learning develops.

Rather than focussing on developmental milestones, and the development of specific physical skills displayed by two-year-old children. The chapter will explore the implication of physical movement and sensory stimulation on the holistic development of two-year-old children.

Two-year-old children are naturally physical, running, climbing, jumping and rolling are all intrinsically motivated movement. Managing the challenge of safety and risk-taking against the need for physicality can become a balancing act.

Looking after a physically active two-year-old can be tiring, the temptation to inhibit and reduce levels of physicality could be considered (by some) as an acceptable way to fit in with today's busy world.

Rather than physicality being an accepted part of a two-year-olds life, it is increasingly viewed as challenging and something that needs to be discouraged. This chapter will explore if we are subconsciously allowing our youngest children to succumb to a society that has little understanding and respect for the importance of movement and physical development?

Physical development

Two-year-olds physical development.

What do you know about two-year-old children and their physical development?

What are your assumptions about two-year-olds and their love of movement?

Physical development is frequently viewed as straightforward, a matter of merely charting children against predictable age-related milestones. If we wish our youngest of children to reach their full potential, it is time we acknowledge and accept the interplay between brain and body. To question the importance of physical development and its link to all other areas of development, it is vital that we are aware of the body's holistic role in the learning process.

Point of note

Gross motor skills are the control of large muscles and large movements made with arms, legs feet or body. Crawling, running, jumping are gross motor skills.

Pause for thought

Your own early life physical experiences.

What opportunities for physical movement did you have as a child?

How does that compare with young children today?

How might this impact children's development?

Growing up in the 21st century means spending increasing amounts of time travelling in cars, playing on screens, being strapped into seats and being encouraged to 'sit nicely'. Rather than viewed as a problematic movement and physicality must be considered as learning tools, and recognised as a significant part of a two-year-olds development.

Physical development

In our society, there is a belief that intellect is developed through the mind and exists separately from the body. In contrast Field (2010) identifies a direct relationship between brain development and young children's experiences.

The neural connection

When considering how young children develop and learn, an awareness of the role of the brain and a basic understanding of brain development is essential.

At birth, a baby's brain has billions of neurons present, but they are not fully connected. After birth, the neural connections are ready to grow and strengthen. Neurons have tiny gaps between them, called synapses, as electrical impulses travel across the synapses, the neuron connections begin to develop and grow.

Synapses develop at an extraordinary rate during the first few years of life. Though many synapses become established, many are lost. It is now accepted that the brain works on a 'use it or lose it' basis. Many neuron connections are discarded if they are not used. By the time a child reaches adolescence 50% of the synapses present in the brain will have been dispensed with.

The central nervous system transmits messages to the brain from all parts of the body. How the brain interprets these messages is dependent upon the strength of the neuron connections. Greenland (2000) uses the metaphor of a roadway to describe the neural wiring of a young child's brain and body. She suggested that it is like a road network that is built in response to sensory stimulation and repetitive movement patterns. The road system is built up through sensory stimulation and repetitive movement patterns. If the roadway is not fully built or connected the journey will not happen, or at best it will be bumpy. Without full neurological organisation, the road journey becomes disrupted, meaning a child's development will be disrupted.

Self-initiated movement and physical experience facilitate neural pathway and nerve growth. As babies grasp, reach out and move their arms and legs around, neural pathways form, allowing the roadway between the brain and body to be constructed.

The positive sensory feedback from this play encourages the baby to repeat the action. Repetition of the movement continues to strengthen the neural pathways between the brain and body. The more young children engage in play, language and physical activities, the stronger and more refined the connections become resulting in the 'building of a superhighway' (Hannaford 2005: 25).

A further feature of brain development is myelination. Myelin is a fatty substance that acts as an insulator supporting the transmission of impulses across the synapses. The experiences and stimulation of young children again in their early years affects the development of myelin and future learning. The importance of early childhood experiences cannot be underestimated, because by the time children start attending preschool their brains are almost fully grown.

> ### Observation: building the connections
>
> Laura (27 months) unhooked an apron, placed it over her head and joined the other children and a member of staff at the water tray. Laura's involvement at the water tray lasted for several minutes, during which time she selected a variety of small-sized receptacles and jugs. She continued to pour water from the jug to the receptacle. Once full, it was discarded, and a new receptacle was selected. The action was then repeated. Laura used both her left and her right hand to hold and pour the water from the jug.
>
> Discussion:
>
> Through her interest and involvement and the repeated movements and practice, her neural pathways will continue to develop and allow her to become proficient in her chosen play (Hannaford 2005). The connections between the body and the mind provide young children with the ability to learn. Laura's interest in pouring and filling and her subsequent knowledge of volume and capacity are reliant on her physical ability to manipulate small containers.

Sensory experiences

Sensory-motor experiences are considered crucial for building early neural development. Exploring and experiencing the material world initiates initial sensory patterns. These develop to become the core of our information systems or the wiring system within us.

Two-year-old children are biologically driven to seek out the sensory-motor experiences that are beneficial for their development. Through the sensory experiences of touching, tasting, smelling, hearing and exploring the environment around them, young children can build their body awareness and construct information and ideas about the world.

Providing suitable outdoor clothing enables two-year-old children to enjoy the sensory experience of puddles, raindrops, wind and snow. The delight, pleasure and joy young children gain from these experiences, enhances the frontal lobes of the brain, forming the foundations for regulating their emotions. It is from these experiences young children develop the ability to manage their feelings, build resilience and gain self-esteem.

Physical development

> **Pause for thought**
>
> Sensory experiences.
>
> What sensory activities are provided as part of your core provision?
>
> What sensory experiences are young children able to freely access?
>
> Are children encouraged to use all their body parts to explore the sensory experiences?
>
> Are indoor and outdoor sensory experiences valued equally?

Movement

Movement activates the neural wiring throughout the body, making the whole body a tool for learning (Hannaford 2005). When a young baby grasps at an object or sucks on an object, they gain sensory feedback, helping them to construct an understanding of the object. Every movement they make is a sensory event that can be linked to their knowledge of our physical world.

Two-year-old children naturally possess the language of movement. When they look at an aeroplane in the sky, their whole body looks up; when they look down at a bug, their entire body moves with them. Movement initiates brain activity, and neural integration occurs. The door to learning opens naturally; it just takes movement.

> **Pause for thought**
>
> Movement opportunities.
>
> How are opportunities for movement provided as part of your provision?
>
> How are children encouraged to use different body parts in their movement activities?
>
> Are indoor and outdoor movement experiences valued equally?

Getting started with reflection

> **Points for practice**
>
> Reduce furniture to provide floor space for children to move
> Encourage young children to spend time on the floor on their tummy when listening to stories or looking at books
> Provide opportunities for walking, running, skipping, jumping, crawling, balancing, step climbing, bike riding, pulling, pushing, throwing, hanging and swinging
> Provide resources for digging in the sand or soil
> Ball play; throwing, catching, rolling and kicking
> The use of action rhymes, music and dancing
> Paint with water on walls and floors

Young children *need* to experience particular sensor motor stimulation, to establish physical development patterns. Misunderstandings about the importance of whole body awareness and its necessity in the lives of young children, often means that sensory experiences are focussed on hands and fingers rather than the entire body.

> *Most of us miss some parts of the pattern. Life isn't perfect, and many factors get in the way – a cold scratchy floor just when we need to creep on our bellies; being held in loving arms when we need to be down on the floor; being put in baby walkers, bouncers and car seats when we need to be crawling sitting still at school when we need to be running, rolling, spinning and hopping; and some of us are even restricted by the instructions to keep tiny designer clothes and shoes clean* (Greenland 2000: 16).

Cephalo–caudal development (muscular control) follows a top-down pattern. Starting with an infant learning to hold their head, the muscle development continues down the body, through the spine to hips, legs and feet.

Young children who frequently put shoes on the wrong foot are demonstrating a lack of sensory feedback from their lower body, they have not yet reached the 'superhighway' level (Hannaford 2005) and, as a result, these children need to explore further sensory experiences with their feet.

Proximodistal development is the process of motor control forming from the centre of the body outwards to the distant parts. In young children, the hands' and fingers' control develops last. The shoulder muscles gain strength and power, then the elbow, wrist hand and finally the fingers.

Physical development

Figure 3.1 Putting on shoes

The development of bilateral coordination allows young children's hands to move separately, one hand may hold an object while the other is manipulating a tool. Some two-year-old children will start to have a preferred hand, they may however, still alternate, especially if they are getting tired or have weak hand strength.

Two-year-old children are still developing dexterity and flexibility in their fingers. A two-year-old child, who holds a pencil by folding their fingers around to enclose it in a vertical position within their hand, is described as using a palmar grasp. The muscles in the shoulder and arm rather than the hand and fingers are controlling the movement of the pencil. As proximodistal development continues to evolve, greater strength and stamina will emerge in the hands than fingers.

Young children will move through several types of pencil grasps before the correct dynamic tripod grasp emerges. It is essential to acknowledge the ability to hold a pencil correctly is linked to a child's physical development and not merely a skill that can be taught.

Getting started with reflection

Figure 3.2 Palmar grasp

Points for practice

Provide a wide range of mark-making resources.

Encourage large arm movement, large vertical and horizontal brush strokes.

Provide activities to promote the pincer movement; the use of the index finger and thumb or thumb and middle finger.

Introduce toys for stacking, threading and pulling apart – blocks, simple jigsaws, threading beads, finger puppets toy cars, animals and dolls.

Give children opportunities to strengthen their hands through holding and squeezing objects.

Physiologically it takes many years for refined movements in the hand (fine motor skills) to fully develop, while these processes cannot be rushed, it is important to ensure two-year-old children's physical development is not constructed or hindered by 21st century practices.

We are all familiar with the five senses that interpret information from outside the body. Yet may not be so familiar with the significance of the vestibular system and the proprioceptive receptors. These two sensory receptors play a vital role in a two-year-olds ability to understand and learn about the spacial position of their body.

Physical development milestones

Most two-year-olds learn to do things like these by the end of their third year:

Gross motor skills

- Walk, run and start learning to jump with both feet
- Pull or carry toys while walking
- Throw and kick a ball; try to catch with both hands
- Stand on tiptoes and balance on one foot
- Climb on furniture and playground equipment
- Walk upstairs, holding on to the railing; may alternate feet
- Carry a large toy or several toys while walking

Fine motor skills

- Start brushing own teeth and hair
- May pull pants up and down
- Wash hands
- Build a block tower of at least four blocks
- Start attempting large buttons and zipping up (if you start the zip)
- Hold utensils and crayons with fingers instead of a fist, although the grasp still may not be quite right
- Self-feed using a spoon and drink from a cup

Proprioceptors in the muscles and joints enable two-year-old children to be aware of the position of their limbs. The proprioceptive receptors are responsible for interpreting physical sensations, measuring and conveying information about the changes in muscle pressure and movement to the brain. Feedback from the proprioceptors to the brain is the only way for balance and body movements to develop.

Feedback from the proprioceptors is interpreted through the **vestibular** system.

The vestibular system performs the complicated job of interpreting the feedback from the proprioceptors.

The vestibular system is responsible for ensuring that the brain is receptive to an incoming sensory stimulus. Body movement activates the vestibular system, when the body is still the vestibular system shuts down. As the body moves, the brain can update and maintain a map of the body's limbs and their position.

Providing the body and brain with the ability to know where our limbs are at all times. This kinaesthetic sense, the feeling of bodily movement, needs to be considered a 'sixth sense'. Without stimulation, this 'sixth sense' remains unconscious and so leaves a gap in the learning potential.

This can also explain how, when children have growth spurts, they can seem clumsy, not entirely in control of their body and movement.

Observation

Michael (28 months) is playing outdoors walking back and forth up and down across the bridge. After several repetitions, he dropped onto his tummy with his legs straight behind him and belly-crawled to the centre of the bridge.

As Michael reached the centre, the top part of the bridge and his head and shoulders began to descend the other side, he stopped and turned onto his bottom, with his legs straight out in front of him.

He shuffled on his bottom down the bridge and, on reaching the end point, he returned, using the same bottom shuffling motion backwards over the bridge.

Perhaps, as Michael tried to 'belly-crawl' down the other side of the bridge, he realised that he was uneasy about the feel and balance of his body and so changed to a more 'comfortable and familiar' bottom shuffling movement.

As he belly crawled along the bridge his hands, belly, legs and feet are all in contact with the bridge Michael used his whole body as a sensory receptor.

Using the whole of his body as a sensory receptor (Hannaford 2005), this enabled Michael to build up a more complicated 'felt' sense of the experience.

It is not uncommon to hear young children being told to 'Walk properly! You are big now! You do not need to crawl!' The messages that are given out by society quickly support the disembodiment of our young children. Focussing on the education of the mind without acknowledging the role of the body in the learning process. Consequentially, this denies the wholeness and completeness that is required for authentic learning.

Risk-taking

Valuing physical development means allowing two-year-old children to become involved in bouts of intense physical activity. Ensuring young children enjoy activities without placing them in actual danger, is an important role. Climbing frames, slides, tunnels, stacking crates, and balancing all comes with an amount of risk.

Point of note

It is essential to evaluate the hazards and eliminate significant risks. However, it must also be pointed out growing up in an overtly safe environment means children are not able to practice their own risk assessment, this in itself creates a different type of danger.

Knowledge of individual children's abilities and limitations ensures all young children are supported to take appropriate risks in their play: a risky play situation for one child might be different from that of another.

Young children, who are regularly able to engage in physical play, learn to assess their own skills, become savvy about themselves and the environment.

Two-year-olds are still in the process of gaining control over their bodies, they need time, space and adults who respect and understand their need to be physically active. A secure base and strong relationship offered by an attuned adult will ensure young children continue to thrive. Rather than trying to rush young children to the next milestone, we must concentrate on the here and now. Enjoy the active moments together, secure in the knowledge we are actually laying the foundations for future holistic learning.

Getting started with reflection

Future challenge

Take some time to consider and reflect: *How aware are you of children's movement activities and patterns?*

Using a reflective model to guide your reflection. Take some time to consider and reflect. The following prompts illustrate how Gibbs reflective cycle supports and scaffolds the process of reflection.

1. Observe a child's natural movement. Record the observation using either written or photographic methods.
2. Acknowledge your feelings, how did the child's movement and behaviour make you feel?
3. How does the environment impact the child's movement? How does it block or facilitate movement and physicality?
4. What might the child have gained from these experiences? How could these movement patterns support learning?
5. What have you learnt about yourself from this experience? What have you discovered about the child you observed?
6. Going forward, how can you reinforce opportunities for movement in the daily routine?

What have *you* gained from this reflection? Share your thoughts and ideas with colleagues.

Communication and language development

Competent communicators

The complexity and importance of communication and language development mean it should not be left to chance. Communication and language 'form the foundation for interacting with other people – for communicating our needs, our thoughts and our experiences' (DCFS 2008: 3).

When we talk about communication and language development, we are talking about speech, the verbal means of using communication and language. Successful verbal communications require putting together sounds to express thoughts and feelings. It is vital those who work and interact with young children have a clear understanding of language development. As it is only through this knowledge, we can enhance our ability to respond, interact, and stimulate young children's language and communication skills.

While different theoretical approaches try to establish how young children learn a language, whether it is innate (nature) or acquired (nurture). The focus of this chapter is not to debate these, but to offer practical knowledge, ideas and guidance to those who work with and support two-year-old children's language development.

It is accepted that from birth on, children are programmed to develop speech and language. The first five years are the most critical, but language development continues throughout early childhood and on into adolescence. During the first five years, stimulation of language development is essential as the brain is developing new nerve cells as well as multiple connections between nerve cells to serve the function of both expressive and receptive language. Severe lack of stimulation during this time can result in children making slower progress, possibly even ending up with weaker communication skills.

Anyone who has tried to communicate in a new language will agree on how difficult this can be. Using spoken language to communicate successfully is complex.

- It requires the production of the correct sounds to produce meaningful words.
- An understanding of the words and there meaning.
- To understand how to order these words; the correct use of grammar to express the intended meaning.

> **Point of note**
>
> While milestones of development will be acknowledged it is essential to recognise that all children are unique and development patterns can be different for all children.

Within the first couple of years of life, most children can express themselves and are well on their way to being competent communicators.

This chapter will discuss the skills and competencies two-year-old children are required to master in order to become competent communicators.

> **Pause for thought**
>
> Communication and language development.
>
> What are your assumptions of two-year-old children and their communication skills?
>
> What do you consider are the challenges of supporting young children's communicating and language development?

Beginning to communicate

Young children are not born with the facility to speak, the word 'infant' actually means 'unable to speak'. From birth babies start to communicate, listening and looking and responding to people and the environment. Gesture, inflexion and emphasis on sounds are all used to communicate children's earliest needs. As Forbes (2004: 110) explains 'long before the use of oral language begins, babies are using all their senses to play with us, to communicate with us.'

Communication and language development

The ability to understand and be understood cannot be underestimated. Early nonverbal communication is the basis for language development. As young children become more experienced at articulating sounds and using single words, the use of gestures often reduces. Young children's ability to develop language skills depends on being immersed in a stimulating environment of words, sounds, rhythm and nonverbal expressions.

> **Pause for thought**
>
> The development of spoken language.
>
> What do you know about young children's language development?
>
> How do you support young children's use of spoken language?
>
> What activities do you do specifically to support language development?

Becoming proficient with spoken language is a huge developmental milestone for young children to achieve. It is essential to be aware of where individual children are within their developmental progress if we are going to be effective in supporting this critical journey.

Spoken language

Acquiring the skills of spoken language involves the development of various skills and knowledge, most of which need to be gained from lived experiences. Most of the actions that take place between young children and adults are supported through the use of language, dressing, lunchtime, nappy changing, will all include a spoken exchange.

To use spoken language, children need to *make* links between the sounds they hear and the meanings of the objects. Initially, the pronunciation of some words can be tricky for two-year-old children they frequently mispronounce words such as *nana for a banana*, many adults recognise this difficulty and provide simplifications of individual words *'nan' for grandma*.

Getting started with reflection

First published in 2008 Every Child a Talker (ECAT) (DCSF) was designed to help create environments to stimulate and support language development. ECAT provided a range of materials including audit tools for evaluating current language provision and identifying priorities for improvement. The following activity is suggested as part of the ECAT audit. The activity can be completed by an individual or as a team. The activity aims to develop confidence, initiate discussion and sharing of ideas and understanding of individual children's language development.

Think about all of the children in your Early Years setting and how they express themselves or communicate. Every child is different, although children can share similarities. Some of the 'types' of communicators you may have in your setting are listed below (you may be able to think of more or different categories).

Early communicator: a child whose communication needs to be interpreted by adults, e.g., a baby who is crying because she is hungry.

Attentive communicator: a child who is using some gestures and some words to communicate, e.g., pointing and saying 'mummy gone'.

Developing communicator: a child who can communicate but finds it difficult to make sentences or pronounce some sounds in words.

Questioning communicator: a child who uses simple sentences to communicate and asks questions to find out more.

Skilled communicator: a child who communicates in the way that you would expect for his/her age.

English as an additional language learner: a child who can communicate effectively in their own language but has not yet learned English.

Reluctant communicator: a child who needs lots of encouragement to communicate or who is 'shy', but is otherwise a competent communicator.

Try to place each of the children in your setting under one of these headings. Which children do you think you are supporting well in their speech and language development? Which children are making good progress? Underline their names in red.

Which children need more support than is currently provided? Underline their names in blue.

Source: Every Child a Talker: Guidance for Early Language Lead practitioners (DCSF 2008: 11) Core activity

Children's early words will be linked to familiar and important people, animals and food; *Mum, dog, milk cup, coat, car ...*

Two-year-old children are usually able to use speech to represent simple actions and consequences; *look, all-gone, hot, bye-bye* (often accompanied by actions). This is because young children's comprehension develops ahead of their productive vocabulary. So they can understand the meaning of words before they can speak them.

> **Pause for thought**
>
> Consider a child who uses less spoken language to communicate.
>
> How have you supported this child today?
>
> What can you do differently to support this child's spoken language development?
>
> How can you further develop your practice to ensure all children benefit?

> **Points for practice**
>
> *The more new words young children hear, the more new words they will learn, and the better they get at talking.*
>
> *Use everyday activities to make connections between actions and objects and the words that represent them.*
>
> *Offer choices, such as 'Do you want an orange or an apple?' Showing the object helps to make the experience more concrete assisting young children in storing a picture of the word in their mind.*
>
> *Simplify your speech when you talk with two-year-old children. Use short sentences and emphasise key words. This will help young children to focus on crucial information.*
>
> *Regularly share books, take time to talk about the pictures, this provides opportunities for listening and developing conversations.*
>
> *Talk with children as much as possible as you go about your daily routine. Ensure you ask simple questions and give time for the child to reply.*

> *When children use two or three words for example 'cup more milk'. Expand this, posing the question 'Do you want some more milk in your cup?'*
>
> *From time to time use sentences that are about one word longer than the sentences children are using. If the child uses two-word sentences, use lots of three and four-word sentences when talking back. For example, if a child says 'a dog' reply 'yes a black dog'.*

Language development is a complex process starting from birth, it develops rapidly during the first few years of life. During this time children must learn to identify and manipulate the sounds to form individual words and eventually a string of words. The sounds that make up a specific language are called *phonemes*, children's phonological development starts as they begin to hear and use the sounds produced in spoken language.

For young children, the challenge of producing and using new words (phonological development) is more complicated than the memory recognition task of comprehending the understanding of words. Two-year-old children understand the meaning of words but have not yet developed the ability to use these words in their speech verbally.

Speaking requires the use of over 100 muscles within the mouth. Articulating sounds (phonemes) correctly is a complex process; most two-year-olds cannot yet fully control the muscles within their mouth and tongue. So affecting the pronunciation and clarity of speech they produce. Familiar adults frequently compensate for this by developing an ear and a better understanding of what a young child is trying to say.

Practice point

It must be acknowledged that all children's development is unique. However, it is imperative we are aware of the children in our care who use less spoken language in their communications with us.

Typically most 20-month-old children will have a spoken vocabulary consisting of between 30–50 words. This will swiftly increase to 300–500 words by the time they turn three years old. Three to four-word utterances become common for two-year-olds. It is common for children to leave out the words that lack meaning to them, 'George shoo', which means George's shoe, this is known as telegraphic speech.

Communication and language development

> **Points for practice**
>
> When listening to young children's speech. It is essential to recognise the sounds (phonemes) they can pronounce. Some are more easily pronounced p, b, m and w are regularly heard within a two-year-olds speech.
>
> In contrast the sounds l, r, w, y, f, th, s, sh, ch, dz, j are more challenging to pronounce, two-year-olds will regularly say *dat* rather than *that*, such speech immaturities are part of the normal phonological development for two-year-olds.

The rules of spoken language

Two-year-old children are also starting to gain an understanding of the use of grammar within spoken language; the rules of spoken language, and how to structure spoken language. Two-year-olds will begin to adjust their speech as they communicate with others.

This is demonstrated as they start to recognise that the order of the words affects the meaning conveyed, and to convey more important details, more words are required. Such as *'George's coat on'*, meaning this is George's coat, and he wants to put it on.

Table 4.1 Stages of Early Speech, Language and Communication Development and Supporting Parental

2–3 years age milestone	*Caregiving behaviours that support the milestone 2–3 years*
Understanding of words and phrases grows quickly during this time.	Build on children's talk, e.g. child: 'Dog!', adult: 'Yes, a big dog'.
Children of this age understand between 200–500 words.	Tap out the beat to songs and rhymes.
Use 'no' or 'not' in phrases.	When playing with your child, give a running commentary on what they are doing, using action words, describing words, position words and feelings as well as object words.
Refers to past/future events.	
Asks questions, e.g. 'What's that?'	
Can pick out objects by function, e.g. Which one do we drink from?	Engage in conversations about feelings and important memories.
Uses pronouns 'I', 'me' and 'you'.	Encourage the child to talk about the future and anticipate events.
Uses descriptive concepts, e.g. big/little.	

The English language is complicated. It has many rules and many exceptions that have to be recognised and followed. Young children not only have to learn the rules, but they also have to learn the exceptions, and this requires both time and experience.

It is common for two-year-olds to apply regular rules to words that change irregularly. For example *'go'* is spoken as *'goed'* rather than went, or *'drinked'* instead of *'drank'*. When young children initially apply a past tense *'ed'* to their speech, it is common to hear it being used to everything; *I runned away; I dranked my milk.*

Actions Source: EIF Early Intervention Framework with Input from National Literacy Trust and Royal College of Speech and Language Therapists.

Correct grammar has to be learned, two-year-old children need scaffolding through this process, it is only through practice and experience that young children learn how to apply the rules of grammar within their speech correctly.

Focused Reflection Point

How do two-year-old children use grammar?

Using a reflective model to guide your reflection. Take some time to consider and reflect children's spoken language skills and their use of grammar. The following prompts illustrate how Kolb's reflective cycle supports and scaffolds the process of reflection.

1. Experience: Take time to consider an individual child's use of grammar in their daily use of language. Also, consider how you respond.
2. Reflect: Think about the situation, does the use of grammar vary across the day? Across different activities. Consider how you respond, how do others respond.
3. Conceptualise: What are your conclusions?
4. Plan: Going forwards how can you scaffold the correct use of grammar? What will you do?

What have *you* gained from this reflection?

The language environment

Abbott and Langston (2005) talk about a warm language environment, suggesting an environment that promotes discussion will include stimulus that provides connections between home and setting. Displaying photographs of children's families and pets, allowing children to independently access and share with others provides strong foundations for the development and practice of communication skills.

Some toys suggested for two-year-olds promise to teach the alphabet or letter names, these toys are frequently glaring in colour and covered in letters and numbers. Resist the temptation young children do not learn abstract concepts in this way. Communication and language development requires real people, real experiences and real conversations.

> **Pause for thought**
>
> The language environment.
>
> How are resources organised?
>
> Do children have free access?
>
> How do you develop links between home and setting?
>
> How and when do children have access to books?
>
> Where is the comfortable space to sit and chat with children?

Children between the ages of two and two and a half can frequently be heard repeating what an adult has said to them. Repeating a word or a phrase several times is called echolalia. **Echolalia** is normal age-related behaviour for two-year-olds, it tends to dissipate around the age of three.

Stammering within speech is not an uncommon occurrence as young children's speech is developing. Stammering occurs when a child hesitates during the speech process, causing several repetitions of a word or sound. **Stuttering** is similar but involves the repetition of a single letter rather than the whole word. This developmental non-fluency is part of young children's developing communication skills and generally should not cause undue concern.

If children exhibit signs of stammering and stuttering, it is vital that adults respond appropriately. Do not try to hurry the speech, or guess what you think the child is trying to say, provide plenty of time, be patient, speak slowly yourself.

> **Point of note**
>
> Signs of stammering and stuttering need to be monitored and shared with parents. In many instances, it will resolve and correct itself.
>
> However, if children become frustrated or it starts to affect their confidence to take part in conversations additional support and referral to speech and language therapy is advisable.

Listening

Young children's ability to listen is not only dependent on their ability to understand language, but it is also linked to brain development. Young children need processing time, listening is an active process, requiring the receiving, interpreting and responding. Young brains need time from hearing the word to recognising and understanding the meaning.

Travarthen and Aitken (1994) suggest two-year-olds brains are more attuned to the intonation and emphasis placed on the specific word than the actual meanings. Asking a two-year-old to help tidy up in a friendly voice, conveys a different meaning than when asked in a frustrated and exasperated voice. Language and communication are inextricably linked to social and emotional development in the life of a two-year-old child.

Spoken language is more natural for two-year-old children to understand if it links to their experiences and interests. Young children often touch or point to an object before they say the word – *George will hold up his wellington boots and shout 'boots on'*. Strong sensory feedback from the object provides a sensory and physical experience that promotes the relationship between thought and language.

Play naturally provides many opportunities for children to practice and develop correct language skills. Two-year-olds will often be heard talking to themselves when they are playing alone, in these scenarios children are using speech and language to help organise and clarify their thinking and understanding of the situation. This self-directed talk is a strategy that many children and some adults continue to use as a way of working through complicated or stressful situations.

Communication and language development

> **Point of note**
>
> Hearing
>
> A key reason why young children's speech and language development is problematic is due to hearing difficulties. Hearing difficulties prevent the sounds of speech being correctly heard. The number of sounds a child might hear can vary daily, so making it difficult for adults to recognise. Hearing impairments can be overlooked, as it is thought the child is simply not concentrating or paying attention.
>
> Signs to look for:
>
> - If you feel they have selective hearing, only hearing when they choose.
> - Slow to respond to instructions.
> - Less intonation or tunefulness in their own voice.

English as an additional language

At this age, children's knowledge of their home language will be in the early stages. It is important to work alongside parents to create high-quality interactions and experiences in both languages. Learning a second language at this age will occur naturally although it can be a little slower to establish.

Having an understanding of language development alongside the confident to provide a language-rich environment, will support the language development of all children. Especially those learning English as a second language.

Getting started with reflection

> **Future challenge**
>
> Take some time to consider and reflect how you support the development of two-year-old children's communication and language skills?
>
> *Using a reflective model to guide your reflection. Take some time to consider and reflect on individual children's communication and language skills. The following prompts illustrate how Kolb's reflective cycle supports and scaffolds the process of reflection.*
>
> 1. Experience: Take time to consider an individual child's communication and language skills. Also, consider what parents say.
> 2. Reflect: Does the use of spoken language vary across the day? Across different activities. Consider how you respond, how do others respond, what do parents say and think?
>
> 3. Conceptualise: What are your conclusions?
> 4. Plan: Going forwards how can you scaffold the development of language skills? What will you do? What can you improve in the environment?
>
> **What have *you* gained from this reflection?** Share your thoughts and ideas with colleagues.

PART 2
The building blocks for learning
The *how* of learning

5 Family life

Over the years the advantages of involving parents in children's learning has been well documented. Nutbrown (2011: 164) insists that 'if children's learning and development opportunities are to be maximized,' professionals must recognise the important and influencing role that parents play within their child's development.

This chapter unpicks the significance and influence family life plays in the young children's development. Suggesting that it is only when parents and professionals work within a collaborative relationship, that children's true achievements will be both understood and acknowledged.

Involving parents in young children's education is not a new concept. Margret McMillian recognised that to improve young children's lives there was a need to also educate the parents. Sharing pedagogy and an understanding of how young children learn 'can be like opening doors to a new world' (Nutbrown 2011: 165).

> **Pause for thought**
>
> Parental involvement.
>
> What do the words 'collaborative relationship' mean to you?
>
> Why do you involve parents in their child's learning?
>
> Why do you share pedagogy with parents?

The building blocks for learning

Parents have a wealth of knowledge about their child. They have spent time watching their child playing, watching them fill and empty toy boxes, or throw balls in the garden. Parents can share information about their child's likes and dislikes, their habits and interest, their fascinations and behaviours.

Collaborative relationships require parents and educator to share their knowledge through piecing together information about the child. Neither the importance, nor the level of skill required to develop such a working relationship with parents can be underestimated.

Cooperation between educator and parent provides the opportunity to develop interpretations and deeper understanding of young children's interests and learning.

Practice points

Treat parents as partners include them in regular discussions about their child's development.
Listen to parents take their views and concerns seriously.
Listening to what parents say about their child's development.
Share your professional knowledge with parents.
Help parents to recognise important milestones of development.
Share educational knowledge and observations about their child's progress.
Help parents to become more involved in their child's learning.
Wherever possible provide resources to loan.
Try to involve parents in decisions regarding their child's learning.

There is no single plan or guide for working with parents, it requires a complex range of skills including sensitivity, empathy and understanding, whilst also having an effective understanding of child development.

Neither the importance, nor the level of skill required to develop such a working relationship with parents can be underestimated. Parents are not a homogenous group; they come with many culturally constructed ideas and beliefs about child development and parenting styles.

Points for action

How can we involve parents? What more can we do? Consider your individual parents

1. Make a key plan outlining different ways to engage parents.
2. Make a list of ideas.

Family life

> 3. Communicate it in any way appropriate for your setting whether through snappy flyers, translated mail-outs, texts, or notice board.
> 4. Never give up hope just because a session fails or no-one turns up; whatever happens, keep going. Vary timings, group sizes, groupings.

Viewing parents as capable and equal partners means understanding the cultural context and how life circumstances will impacts the ability to parent effectively.

Parenting styles can vary amongst different generations and cultures, parents unique beliefs about raising young children often stem from their own family culture.

Parenting styles

Many parents have different ideas about how to raise a child, the differing styles and strategies adopted are known as **parenting styles.**

Parenting styles refers to the combination of strategies used to raise children. During the early 1960s, psychologist Diana Baumrind identified four different parenting styles. Each style is categorised by its use of warmth, nurturing, communication and expectations of maturity and control.

> **Pause for thought**
> Parenting styles.
>
> What do you know about parenting styles?
>
> What different strategies have you observed parents using?
>
> What do you believe are the best strategies to use with two-year-old children?

Authoritarian parents believe children should follow the rules without exception Rules are made and enforced with little regard for a child's opinion.

Authoritarian parents may use punishments instead of discipline. So rather than teach a child how to make better choices, they're invested in making children feel sorry for their mistakes.

Children who grow up with strict authoritarian parents tend to follow rules much of the time. Children of authoritarian parents are at a higher risk of development self-esteem problems because their opinions aren't valued.

Authoritative parents have rules and they use consequences, but they also take their children's opinions into account. They validate their children's feelings while also making it clear that the adults are ultimately in charge.

Authoritative parents invest time and energy into preventing behaviour problems before they start. They believe in using positive strategies to reinforce good behaviour.

Children raised with authoritative discipline tend to be happy and successful. They're also more likely to be good at making decisions and evaluating safety risks on their own.

Permissive parents usually take on more of a friend role than a parent role. They often encourage their children to talk with them about their problems, but they usually don't put much effort into discouraging poor choices or bad behaviour.

Young children who grow up with permissive parents are more likely to struggle academically. They may exhibit more behavioural problems, as they don't appreciate authority and rules. They often have low self-esteem and may report a lot of sadness.

Uninvolved parents tend to have little knowledge of what their children are doing. Children may not receive much guidance, nurturing, and attention.

Uninvolved parents may be neglectful but it's not always intentional. A parent with mental health issues or substance abuse problems, for example, may not be able to care for a young child's physical or emotional needs on a consistent basis.

At other times, uninvolved parents lack knowledge about child development. Sometimes being simply overwhelmed with other problems, like work, paying bills, and managing a household.

Children with uninvolved parents are likely to struggle with self-esteem. They tend to perform poorly in school. They also exhibit frequent behaviour problems and rank low in happiness.

In reality parents often do not fit into just one category, they demonstrate a mix of different styles, chopping and changing strategies as children grow and situations evolve.

However it is clear, **authoritative parenting** is considered the best parenting style, allowing parents to maintain a positive relationship whilst still establishing authority in a healthy manner.

Family life

If we accept that children's development is influenced by the activities and environment they inhabit, then we have to acknowledge that family culture will also be a feature of the places and spaces children inhabit.

The concept of culture as a feature within child development can be difficult to understand and visualise. However, if we consider the influence family life has on

Family life

a child's upbringing, we can start to understand the importance culture plays in the life of a two-year-old.

Taking the premise that two-year-old children are active participants rather than just bystanders and observers in their worlds. Infers that children's development will be facilitated or constrained by families cultural beliefs; the experiences they gain. Two-year-old children's the experiences will be regulated by family culture.

As the primary caregiver, parents play an important role in orchestrating children's experiences 'directly through their beliefs and behaviours and indirectly through the network of relationships they develop within the family and wider society' (Penderi and Petrogiannis 2011: 33).

> **Pause for thought**
>
> Family culture.
>
> What are your assumptions around the concept of culture?
>
> What does the term 'culture' mean to you?
>
> What would be your definition of culture?
>
> What is the significance between culture and child development?
>
> How does culture feature in child development?

When we are asked to consider the concept of culture, issues of ethnicity, faith, language, moral frameworks, or parenting beliefs are often cited as examples or illustrations. Concepts of culture such as ethnicity, faith and language can imply the idea that culture is somehow a fixed entity, something we are born into.

I would like to put forward the view that culture can also be a fluid entity that is built up through everyday human social interaction. Family cultures and beliefs around child development and parenting can be influenced through social interactions with others.

Bronfennbrenner's ecological theory model (1979) can be used to illustrate cultural and environmental influences on young children and their families. This model can be visualised as a set of concentric circles within each other, demonstrating the movement from the most intimate influences in the centre to the more remote context beyond.

The building blocks for learning

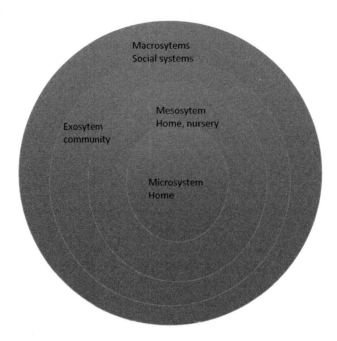

Figure 5.1 Bronfennbrenner's ecological theory

The home environment and family cultural practices is the innermost circle (microsystem). The next circle (mesosytem) represents the extended links outside of the home; the nursery setting, the church, and the parent groups etc. that will have an impact on the child and families experiences of culture.

The following circle (exosytem) represents aspects that have a less direct influence on the child and families first hand experiences, such as the parental work place, community networks, and finally there is the most remote circle (macrosytems), which still has an impact on the family and child's life in the form of social systems, such as the law and economic and educational policies.

Children are most likely to acquire the skills and knowledge that are promoted by their parent's cultural ideas and beliefs. However, social interaction and influences from the outer circles will impact parental practices and beliefs. Put simply, mixing with people that do things in a certain way, or have certain beliefs will (with or without our consent) influence our beliefs and ways of doing things.

Observation Emily: Home Learning environment

Emily was waiting by the front door as I arrive at her house.
Emily soon became involved in the wooden number jigsaw.

Family life

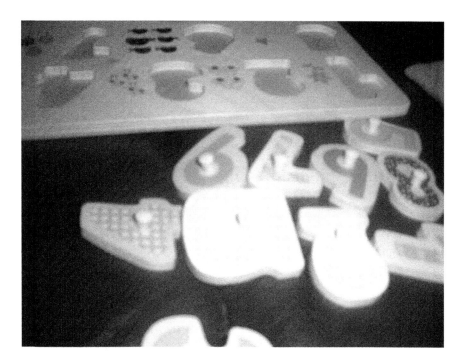

Figure 5.2 Number puzzle

As Emily replaced each piece, she said the number names out loud. Emily's mother confirms, 'She knows the number names, we say them together. I think it is important she knows her numbers. You like 8, 9 and 10, you know they go together.' On completion, Emily gesturing for me to take a photograph of the jigsaw puzzle.

Emily completes the puzzle with ease, whilst also recalling all the number names. This infers that at only 27 months of age, Emily can competently recognise and use number names. In this situation Nutbrown (2011) would explain that Emily's speech, and her knowledge of number names has arisen from her mother's regular and repeated commentary, used to support Emily's actions as she repeatedly completes the puzzle.

Regularity and repetition of parental practices within the child's microenvironment (the home) ensures the core messages are emphasised and repeated. Emily's regular exposure to these messages has influenced her learning. She can now competently resight number names from 0–10.

Emily's acquisition and knowledge of the number names. Illustrates the mediating and shaping role of family culture and its influence within the home learning environment.

Emily's home experiences regularly expose her to opportunities to hear number names, meaning at only two years of age she is able to competently resight and use number names within her play. Emily's exposure and subsequent knowledge of number names demonstrates the powerful and influential role of family culture.

While family culture provides an explanation for Emily's knowledge of number names it also highlights an important need to recognise the knowledge young children bring with them as they enter educational settings.

Home learning environment

The importance of the home learning environment cannot be underestimated. Parental involvement in activities such as reading to their child, visiting the library, playing with letters and numbers, singing nursery rhymes, mark making, have a huge impact on children's achievements.

> ### Points for practice
> Home learning environment. Activities that have the biggest impact are:
>
> - Reading, sharing books and going to the library
> - Going out on visits
> - Playing with print (letters and numbers)
> - Singing songs and nursery rhymes
> - Drawing and painting (making meaningful marks) and playing with friends

It has been recognised while other family factors such as parent's education and socioeconomic status have some relevance, parental involvement within the home learning activities exert a greater and long lasting influence on children's educational attainments.

The quality and diversity of the interactions between the child and their parents will determine the quality of the home learning environment.

> ### Pause for thought
> Parental engagement.
>
> How do you specifically target parental engagement?

> Or do you wait until there appears to be a problem?
>
> How effectively do you encourage parents to support their child's learning in literacy?
>
> How could this be developed further?
>
> How effectively do you encourage parents to support their child's learning in numeracy?
>
> How could this be developed further?

Children's development is enhanced through the home learning environment, not only by involvement in stimulating activities but also and more importantly by developing the child's ability and motivation concerned with learning. The home learning environment is intrinsically linked to young children's feeling of self-esteem and self-confidence, their belief in themselves as a learner. Chapter 6 will look in more detail about developing positive dispositions to learning.

The National Literacy Trust (2018) summarised why home learning matters:

- The quality of the HLE is a key predictor of a child's early language ability and future success; positive experiences can have lasting and life changing impacts.
- Early language ability is consistently linked to later outcomes – including school attainment and job prospects.
- Children raised in middle and upper-income homes are more likely to experience a language-rich environment. By contrast, children from low-income homes are more likely to arrive at school with below-average language skills, leaving them at an educational disadvantage from the start.
- But this is not inevitable. All parents have the power to change outcomes for their children, no matter what their background.
- And we know that behaviour change approaches can work in the family setting; we can help parents to support their children's learning through public programmes, resources, brands, social marketing and broadcasting.

The building blocks for learning

Viewing parents as capable partners and recognising the important and influential role of the home learning environment, only then can the true power of early childhood education be fully recognised.

Only, when parents and professionals work within a collaborative relationship, children's true achievements will be both understood and acknowledged. Identifying the need for practitioners to be both confident and articulate in recognising, understanding and sharing pedagogical knowledge with parents.

> **Challenge for the future**
>
> How do you continue to build collaborative relationship between parents and practitioners?
> How do you support the home learning environment?
> *Using a reflective model to guide your reflection. Take some time to consider and reflect. The following prompts illustrate how Kolbs reflective cycle supports and scaffolds the process of reflection.*
>
> 1. Experience: Take time to recognise the important and influencing role that parents play within their child's development.
> 2. Reflect: Identifying the relationships between parents and practitioners:
>   - How information is shared with parents?
>   - How are parent's ideas and concerns valued?
>   - Have you ever heard staff make judgemental comments about parents?
>   - What changes been made as a result of parental suggestions?
>
> 3. Conceptualise: What are your conclusions? Consider the knowledge you have gained from this chapter.
> 4. Plan: Identify how changes can be made, be realistic change can take time.
>
> **What have *you* gained from this reflection?** Share your thoughts and ideas with colleagues.

6 | Dispositions and mindset

As a profession, we are becoming more aware of the impact the first few years of a child's life has on their future life chances and achievements. With this in mind, we have to look beyond merely ensuring children's early attainment. Our responsibility includes nurturing young children to become active life-long learners. To do this, we must not only understand how young children learn; more significantly we must accept our role in supporting children's development as learners.

Research suggests how children approach learning has a significant impact on their achievement, both in school and future life. Children vary in their belief about their ability to succeed. Some children not only have a strong motivation to learn but also demonstrate greater persistence and resilience within the learning process.

This chapter will explore the role of such traits and dispositions in young children's ability to take charge of their own learning and become leaders of their learning.

> **Pause for thought**
>
> Learning to learn.
>
> What does the term 'leaders of their own learning' mean to you?
>
> How do you support young children to become leaders of their own learning?

The building blocks for learning

Young children are often described as naturally curios and intrinsically motivated to investigate and explore their surroundings. Through a combination of interacting with the environment and support form appropriate adult's, young children can make sense and learn about their own abilities and the material world they inhabit.

Such experiences provide the context and foundation for social and cognitive learning. However, more importantly, such experiences start to build children's own belief about their ability to succeed.

Two-year-old children's thoughts about themselves as learners can be fostered or hindered by their experiences. All adults have a pivotal role in contributing to a young child's perception of their ability to learn.

Point of note

The term **learning dispositions** refer to how learners engage in and relate to the learning process. Learning dispositions affect how children approach learning and therefore the outcomes of their learning.

Early life experiences provide two-year-old children with the opportunity and power to become confident, creative, risk takers, independent, decision makers, motivated, persistent and resilient. Such opportunity allows young children to grow as learners, and more importantly allow adults to 'celebrate children's growth as learners' (Stewart 2011: 17).

Young children and learning

Two-year-old children have to master many **skills**. Learning to walk, run, skip, hop, balance on one leg, counting, sorting, matching are but a few of the many skills young children learn and develop through practice.

Two-year-old children naturally acquire **knowledge** as they go about their daily lives. Asking questions, exploring, observing are all the ways young children gain knowledge and an understanding of the world they live in. Almost without trying young children learn new vocabulary, new concepts, there knowledge of songs and stories increases as their experiences in the world evolve.

The early years of a child's life are an essential time for discovering and learning about our innate emotions. **Feelings** of confidence, security and belonging are all learnt in the early years. Learning about attitude and how to control our feelings starts in early childhood.

Perhaps an aspect of learning that is not so recognised is that of **dispositions**.

Dispositions are the way we respond to certain situations; they can be considered as habits of mind. Dispositions are not learnt through instruction but gained and strengthened through being around others who display and exhibit them.

Dispositions are a combination of young children's emerging skills, knowledge and attitudes to learning. There is a distinct difference between having ball skills and having the disposition to be a professional footballer.

Some of the necessary dispositions for young children to learn are **curiosity, creativity, cooperation, courage, perseverance, confidence, trust** and **responsibility**.

> **Pause for thought**
>
> Learning dispositions.
>
> What do you understand by the term dispositions?
>
> What is a positive learning disposition?

> **Observation**
>
> **Heuristic play: 'stacking'** (Hannah 30 months)
> *Hannah took her time to precisely select a range of resources. She then proceeded to place the smaller objects inside the larger objects, before taking them out and repeating the whole process again and again and again.*
>
> *Her investigation appeared calm, methodical and organised. As the investigation continued Hannah's actions demonstrate her realisation that not all the objects fitted inside each other. Hannah was able to stack some of the resourced on top of each other.*

The building blocks for learning

Figure 6.1 Heuristic play

Hannah spent over 20 minutes exploring the different resources, repeatedly fitting them inside each other and stacking them on top of each other. The nursery room was busy and noisy, but Hannah did not seem to notice, she was thoroughly engrossed in her investigation.

Hannah displays both a positive disposition and a mindset that allowed her to overcome difficulties during her investigation.

Dispositions are the responses two-year-old children display during uncertain learning opportunities and circumstances. Practitioners and adults can support young children to find their way to be successful learners in such situations.

Young children's development as a successful learner can be achieved when praise and value are placed on the methods and strategies adopted by the child, rather than the final result.

Hannah had a positive response when she discovered that not all the resources would fit inside each other. She responded by finding new ways to work with the resources. Hannah's positive disposition and persistence afforded her new learning opportunities; the realisation the resources could also be used for stacking.

Claxton and Carr (2004: 88) use the example of 'persistence', suggesting that, knowingly or not, we influence the strengths of children's inclination and competences. Meaning, if we repeatedly value the effort and persistence a child puts into their play, young children are more likely to repeat these actions.

My own recent experiences in the nursery setting support this view, when children's persistence is highlighted and valued by all adults (educators and parents) children are more inclined to repeat it, for example, several children will now spend time putting on and fastening up their own coat, something they previously would not attempt.

Points for practice

Developing positive dispositions ...

- Display photographs of children who appear competent, e.g. pouring water in the water tray.
- Ensure children have positive interactions with a key worker.
- Provide opportunities for making own choices.
- Provide open-ended resources, with no right or wrong way to play.

Gaining a positive disposition to learning can take time, the actions and response displayed by the child need to be recognised and valued by all adults and peers in the learning community.

For example, when observing a group of two-year-old children involved in a large construction play activity. Positive dispositions to learning can be highlighted by celebrating and recognising particular children's patience and perseverance within the play. Recoding the play episode through photographs allows it to be shared and discussed, the skills of patience and perseverance are illustrated and shared with other children; the learning community is demonstrating its recognition and value of the learning dispositions.

> **Pause for thought**
>
> Building the learning community.
>
> How do you value the effort and persistence a child puts into their play?
>
> How do you share this with other children and adults?
>
> What can you do to further this?

Dweke's (2015) research is fascinating and informative. She believes the subliminal messages adults give to children can influence their developing mindset. Praising children by saying things like 'you're a natural!' or 'you are a brilliant artist' can lead to the belief that being good at something is out of their control.

Point of note

Professor Carol Dweck, a psychologist on the faculty at Stanford University describes those individuals who take control of their learning as having a **growth mindset**. Believing that their ability and intelligence can be improved if they try harder, in contrast, she describes individuals who think ability or intelligence cannot be changed as having a **fixed mindset**; these individuals believe there is nothing they can do about their performance.

Children will begin to believe that they succeeded in something merely because they are gifted. As they want to maintain this image and continue to look good in front of others, such children will begin to worry about failing or not doing as well next time. This may mean they repeat activities they are confident with, rather than taking risks in their learning, as they believe this may cause them to lose their high-performance label.

In contrast, focusing praise on the effort, or the strategy demonstrated by the child can induce very different results. Praising children by saying things like 'you have put so much effort into this', or 'I can see you have practised'. Helps to develop children's resilience to failure as it teaches them what to do when they are challenged or fail – try again, try harder or try a different way, all things that are within their control.

This type of praise is sometimes called 'process praise', Dweke's (2015) research found that children were more motivated when their parents used more of this kind of praise.

> A **fixed mindset** occurs when we believe abilities and traits are fixed; we have no control over them; we are born with them. In contrast, those who think their abilities can be changed and developed through learning, practice, persistence and hard work would be described as having a **growth a mindset**.

A growth mindset attaches success to the learning process, allowing young children to believe that new skills and knowledge can be learnt. The learner recognises that intelligence and abilities can be developed through effort, persistence, trying different strategies and learning from mistakes. Children as young as two-years quickly understand, if they practice putting on their coat, they get better at it.

Children with a fixed mindset will tend to give up on challenging tasks or even avoid tasks they have found difficult in the past. Unfortunately, they believe being 'good' at something is a fixed talent, and something they have no control over. Over time children who feel like this often reduce their effort, and may even display negative behaviour to detract from the fact they are struggling – possibly leading to low self-confidence and self-worth.

In contrast children (and adults) with a growth mindset think very differently. They understand they can get better by practising, when they face a challenge, they become more determined to succeed, overcoming setbacks through their determination and perseverance. Hard work and failure is seen as part of the learning process and does not threaten them.

Pause for thought

Fixed and growth mindset: consider the children in your setting.

Can you identify children with a fixed and growth mindset?

How can you develop a growth mindset for children?

How will you reduce the fixed mindset for children?

Developing a growth mindset

We often talk about developing our muscles, getting strong muscles to help us lift and move heavy objects. Explain to young children that our brains are like our muscles, the more we use it, the stronger they get, the better we become at thinking. The more we work and practice the better we get when young children meet a challenge, encourage them to keep trying, to find another solution, to keep practising; working hard grows our brains.

It is crucial young children realise making mistakes is all part of the learning process when mistakes happen, celebrating how they were overcome sends out powerful messages to the learning community about what type of learning is valued.

Point for action

Growth and fixed mindsets affect both children and adults, consider your responses to the following questions.

Watch for a fixed-mindset reaction when you face challenges. Do you feel overly anxious, or does a voice in your head warn you away? Watch for it when you encounter a setback in your teaching, or when students aren't listening or learning. Do you feel incompetent or defeated? Do you look for an excuse? Watch to see whether criticism brings out your fixed mindset. Do you become defensive, angry, or crushed instead of interested in learning from the feedback? Watch what happens when you see an educator who's better than you at something you value. Do you feel envious and threatened, or do you feel eager to learn? Accept those thoughts and feelings and work with and through them. Moreover, keep working with and through them (Dweke 2015).

We live in an ever-advancing world, the future has endless possibilities for the young children of today.

Future Challenge

The activity can be completed by an individual or as a team. The activity aims to develop confidence, initiate discussion and sharing of ideas and understanding around the development of positive dispositions for learning with two-year-old children.

Using a theoretical reflective cycle or develop your own model, take some time to consider; **how to create two-year-old children's dispositions to learning**. *The following questions may help to guide your reflection.*

- How do you offer a challenge as part of daily routines for two-year-old children?
- How do you recognise and support the challenge in two-year-old children's play?
- How do you share this with children and parents?

What have you gained from this activity? Share your thoughts and ideas with colleagues.

7 Key person

Two-year-olds have a desire to explore and a craving for independence combined with their naturally impulsive nature and frequent lack of self-control together with their many emotional displays and outbursts; render the 'terrible twos' a challenging time.

Viewing the world from a two-year-olds perspective provides greater insight and understanding, and with this new knowledge and understanding comes the confidence to compromise and negotiate rather than try to control and maintain power over two-year-olds.

Two-year-olds require a considerable amount of attention requesting patient empathetic and sensitive responses from those who are close to them.

> **Pause for thought**
>
> Working with two-year-old children.
>
> What excites you?
>
> What concerns do you have?

In England, it is now a statutory requirement that all children in the Early Years Foundation Stage (DfE 2018) have a key person. While seemingly a straightforward requirement, this chapter will explore some of the implications and considerations of

The building blocks for learning

implementing a successful key person approach for two-year-old children and their families.

The key person approach is not a system or a rota or an organisational tool that can be imposed. An effective key person approach is an on-going commitment to put young children's needs at the centre of our practice. Part of the key person approach will include the struggle to overcome the challenges and make it work. Being able to hear and respond to the voices, wishes and feelings of young children (Elfer et al. 2003).

In the nursery setting the key person is responsible for developing and maintaining the relationships with the children and their family.

The key person builds and continues the relational bonds becoming the special person and safe base for the child during their time in the nursery.

The key person is the foundation for the child's personal, social and emotional developmental journey.

> **Pause for thought**
>
> What qualities do you have that will make you a successful key person?
>
> What do you enjoy about this role?
>
> What are the challenges to this role?

The quality of the key person relationship has a direct bearing on young children's potential to learn, inexperienced or staff who respond only to a child's physical needs will impact on the level of stress the child experiences. Exposure to stress can be dangerous for young children; the stress hormone cortisol can interfere with brain growth and development.

The physical, emotional and intellectual demands of looking after and caring for someone else's child are considerable and complex. Displayed through their desire to maintain close proximity, two-year-olds will want to stay physically close to their key person. Frequently returning to seek reassurance through the physical contact of a hug or cuddle. As children mature they become more self-reliant returning for a chat, to share play episodes or engage in play with their key person.

Key person

Strong key worker relationships take time to develop; it is dependent on not just the time spent together, but also the quality of the experiences shared between key worker and child.

The key person role is complex; it requires warmth, fun loving and sensitive adults who are fully available and committed to respond to the child's emotional needs.

> **Pause for thought**
>
> Consider your key children.
>
> How do they communicate with you?
>
> What signals do you look out for?
>
> How do individual children differ in their needs for reassurance?

When two-year-old children feel confident with their key person, they are more likely to seek them out and spend quality time together; in return, this has an impact on young children's communication and language development. The key person becomes attuned with their children if early speech is not clear; the key person is often the only adult that can understand and make sense.

> **Point of note key person role involves**
>
> - Building attachments and get to know the child.
> - Assisting both parent and child during the settling in period.
> - Building a strong relationship with parents and families.
> - Providing parents with information regarding the routines, daily time-tables, and activities in the room.
> - Supporting the child in becoming familiar with the daily routine and the layout of the nursery.
> - Being aware of circumstances at home that may affect changes in a child's behaviour from time to time.

The building blocks for learning

- Organising key person time, in small groups or one to one time every day.
- Closely monitoring the child's progress in all areas of development.
- Knowledge of each child's needs for planning activities and curriculum.

Getting to know each other

Sharing information about yourself with parents is the first step in building relationships. Many nurseries use a staff board to inform parents about the nursery staff team.

While knowledge of qualifications is essential parents also want to learn about the human side of who is caring for their child, information about pets, sports hobbies etc. can provide a connection for future story sharing.

It is crucial that parents understand the importance of settling young children into the nursery, it may be necessary to share knowledge about attachment theory and separation anxiety to help parents understand the importance of getting 'it right'.

The parent also needs to understand and accept their role in the settling in process, if they do not feel confident their child will pick up on this. The secure attachments two-year-old children have with their parent means they can quickly become distressed if they are separated; this, in turn, can make it challenging to introduce new environments and people.

Observation tuning in: Emily 25 months

Emily spotted her key person (Leanne) and joined her at the water but Emily joined in the play. She selected a container and proceeded to fill it with water and then tipped it out. Leanne narrated Emily's actions, as she repeated and further explored the movement of the water.

Leanne: Emily is tipping the water ... Can you see the water ... the water falls down ... Can you do it again ... Emily makes the water fall again.

Emily quickly became absorbed with the activity.

When Leanne moved away, Emily chose to remain and continue her water play.

Ignoring the advancement from a different staff member who joined the water play Emily moved to rejoin Leanne indoors. Leanne was helping the younger children on the slide. Emily joined in. She patiently waited to take her turn to climb up the steps and then walked down the slope of the slide.

Leanne moved away, and Emily remained at the slide, repeatedly climbing up the steps and walking down the slope. Emily began to narrate her actions

> *Emily is on the slide ... Emily can go up and down ... Emily at the top ... Emily at the bottom.*
>
> *After many trips up and down the slide on her feet, Emily announced, 'I sit'. She then proceeded to slide down the slide on her bottom, repeating this action many times.*
>
> Emily's relationship with her key worker: it can be clearly observed that Emily appears to ignore the support from the less well-known adult, choosing instead to seek out her key person. Elfer et al. (2003: 23) visualise this as 'an elastic thread of attachment that allows for being apart as well as for being together.'
>
> Leanne has come to know Emily and as such cannot only respond but also anticipate her interests and needs.

New situations

Settling young children into a nursery can be difficult. Separation anxiety is a normal response from any young child, making it imperative that before young children are separated from their parents, they need the opportunity to build a relationship with their key person.

It is essential to find out about the child, knowing about their personality and prior experiences of separating from parents will help you to make a unique settling in plan.

- It is vital to have a flexible approach to settling in visits.
- Some children will need several visits while others often sibling of children already attending may need less as they are already familiar with you.

A successful **settling in process** is the result of parents and key person working together. Allowing the key person to start forming a relationship with their child means parents must feel confident to withdraw gradually.

Realising that this may require 5 or 6 visits can be a shock for some parents, in my experience, it is best to provide written information with an explanation of each stage of the settling in process.

Building the attachment relationship

Settling in visits are all about building attachment between the child and the key person, the child getting to know the key person; the key person familiarising themselves with the child. As previously explained in Chapter 1 it takes time to build attachments; settling in visits cannot be rushed or fast-tracked. It is essential that parents are made aware of this when they organise the nursery start date.

The building blocks for learning

> **Points for practice**
>
> Find out from parents.
>
> - What separation experience have parents and child had so far?
> - Has the child been left with close family – how did this go?
> - Has the child been to another setting – crèche?
> - Are there siblings? How well did they settle into the nursery?
> - How outgoing and confident is the child?
> - How does the child show anxiety? Thumb sucking.
> - Find out about likes and dislikes.
> - Find out about home routines.
> - Favourite/familiar song or story.
> - Encourage parents to chat with the nursery team and leave with a smile and a kiss.

During the **initial settling in visit**, it is important that the child, parent and key person have time together to play, demonstrating to the child that the parents trust the key person. It is essential that the parent remains present but allows the key person to respond to the child during the play. Acknowledging the key person to be the sensitive adult who can respond to the child's signals.

The next stage in the settling in process is about increasing the physical proximity between child and parent. Once play has been established between the child and the key person, the parent retreats a short distance away from the child.

Initially, the key person can explain 'mummy has gone to get the book from the cupboard', it is important the child is aware of what is going on and can continue to play. The security offered by the key person needs to be strong enough to not just prevent distress, but also that the child feels secure and confident of maintaining their trail of thought, their play.

Moving out of the child's line of sight is an essential and often difficult step in the settling in process. Once play between the child and key person is established the parent moves out of sight from the child to a different part of the room. It is essential that the child can continue with their play; at this moment the child is now dependent on the key person for security and reassurance.

> **Point of note**
>
> While the settling in visits are primarily arranged and organised around the child's needs, they will also support the parent's separation anxiety. Vitally the visits allow parents to get to know and build trusting relationships with nursery staff.

Once children are comfortable and allow parents to move out of view, the next stage of settling in requires children to enable parents to leave the nursery building. This will involve saying good-bye and watching a parent go through the door. This can be an emotionally troubling time for both parent and child.

Once the child and key person are settled and playing, the parents need to confidently explain they are nipping out, and will soon be back. The parent then needs to walk confidently to the door and leave the nursery. The key person can help the child say 'bye mummy' reassuring that 'mummy will soon be back' if the child follows to the door, key person continues to reassure 'mummy nipping to get something she will soon be back', it is essential to not restrain the child, to comfort and redirect their attention.

Initially, the parent needs to only leave for a few minutes; this needs repeating over several move visits, as the child becomes more comfortable the period can gradually increase.

I would advise that settling in visits take place at different times during the day, as this also allows the child to observe and experience the various routines of the session. Young children can appear to be settling into the nursery but show anxiety around having their nappy changed or going to the toilet; this needs to be experienced during the settling in visits. Visiting the bathroom together allows the parent to initiate the nappy change and the key person to take over and complete.

Sleeping on mats or in bags on the floor will not be something most children are familiar with, having their parent or carer stay for the first time will help to give reassurance.

Transition times within a session can cause anxiety to some young children, tidying up can be noisy and disruptive times. Initially, as children are settling in, ensure your proximity before any transition time, offering support and diverting any unnecessary distress at these times.

> **Pause for thought**
>
> Look back on your day at work.
>
> What were the stressful parts?

Why were these stressful?

What could be done differently to reduce the stress?

Now consider the day from a child's perspective, would your answers be any different?

Continuing the journey

While it may be inevitable that some children experience emotional distress it is vital that nursery rules and boundaries are appropriate, and not just because 'we have always done it this way'! Rules need to be regularly evaluated and discussed between staff to ensure validity and consistency in approach from all staff.

Point of note

If, during any part of the settling in process children or parent becomes upset and display anxiety it is essential to take a step back, to slow the process down, allowing more time for the relationship between child key person and parent to consolidate.

It is crucial that children's experiences of separation are positive. If a two-year-old experiences on-going separation anxiety it will become part of their unconscious memory. Experiencing separation or transitions later in life can reignite this memory causing additional emotional distress. Increasing numbers of older primary aged children are displaying behaviours related to attachment and separation anxiety.

On occasion, young children's behaviour can elicit adults to feel strong emotions; on these occasions, it is essential to step away to reflect on the experience. Nursery's that have a culture of reflection and open discussion enable practitioners to develop a new understanding and knowledge of young children's behaviour.

> **Pause for thought**
>
> Is there behaviour displayed by young children that particularly bothers you?
>
> How do these make you feel?
>
> Why do you think this might be?

Most two-year-olds do not yet have the skills to speak fluently, the way they behave is their means of communicating. If things go wrong and they feel uneasy or frustrated, this will often be reflected in their actions and behaviour. At times of stress, young children are physically unable to regulate their behaviour. It is essential to accept that while a two-year-olds behaviour can be challenging to manage at times, it is appropriate for the age.

Biting is a typical behaviour seen in young children between the ages of 18 months to two and a half years. Dealing with age-appropriate behaviour is not easy.

When biting occurs: stay calm, do not be tempted to let your feelings show, it is essential not to give the child who has bitten any attention. The child must not learn they can gain adult attention for this action.

Make sure both children are safe – focus on the child who has been bit – the victim. Avoid focusing any attention on the child who has done the biting, this includes eye contact.

Look after the victim, check the damage and treat appropriately along with plenty of warmth care and reassurance.

A child who has bitten once will bite again; two-year-old children have very little control over their reactions and actions when put under pressure. Talking about what they have done or asking them not to do it again is pointless.

The focus needs to be on prevention; try to identify the trigger; it is essential not to put the child back into the same situation as their learnt response will be to bite again.

Triggers can include:

- Feeling tired or hungry.
- Frustration – wanting a toy from another child.

For the remaining nursery session, the child who has bitten needs to remain next to their keyworker. They must be kept busy and occupied in my experience; it is also best to keep them away from the child they have bitten. It is important to not discuss

The building blocks for learning

or reflect on the biting incident with a two-year-old, instead focus on keeping them involved and at your side.

The parental and key person relationship can come under pressure, as a result of this situation most parents will be upset to find out their child has bitten. Parents may also need support and reassurance that this is typical age-related behaviour. It is best, to be honest with parent sharing future strategies and find out if such incidents have occurred at home.

The focus on prevention must continue over the next few nursery sessions.

It is crucial to prevent any further opportunities for the child to become frustrated and repeat the behaviour, ensure they remain at all times with an adult, if possible their key person.

If after several days no further biting attempts have been made at home or in the nursery the child can be allowed to play independently of the adult for short periods. It is best to start this in a different place to where the first bite took place and not within proximity to the original victim. At other times engage the child in small group play, with an adult.

An essential part of the key person role is to maintain a relationship with the child and their family. It is necessary to be aware of any changes in a child's home life as this can be reflected in their actions and behaviour.

Talking to the parents of the bitten child can be a tricky conversation, it is essential to be honest, and explain what has occurred. Reassuring parents their child has received appropriate physical and emotional care is essential. In my experience bite marks can look angry, letting parents know in advance may better prepare them, rather than waiting until they collect their child at nursery.

The conversation needs to focus on the strategies the nursery and key person employ to prevent future biting incidents occurring. Providing a copy of the nurseries policy and procedure can give the parents further reassurance about how such incidents are managed.

Pause for thought

Managing two-year-old age-appropriate behaviour.

Do you talk about typical behaviour two-year-olds display?

Is this something you feel confident to talk about with parents?

Small group time; providing organised times for young children and their key person to meet together in a particular place supports opportunities for a sense of belonging and security to flourish. The close proximity can rejuvenate the feeling of safety and trust young children hold for their key person and start to develop relationships with their peers.

The time can be used for singing, storytelling or chatting. I have observed this time used to share photographs taken during the nursery session that morning. The children were not only captivated to see themselves in the photographs, but it provoked conversation about other children's activities.

Photographs are powerful tools; having pictures of children and their family member strategically placed around the nursery room can enhance a child's feeling of security. The key person approach is not about replacing parents but allowing children to develop multiple attachments, acknowledging young children's primary carers will add to a young child's sense of security and belonging.

Toilet training

There are many different ideas about toilet training, making it easy for parents to feel overwhelmed nervous and apprehensive about the whole process. A child's key person should be able to offer advice about their child's readiness.

It is essential that parents understand that you cannot force a child to use a potty. They have to be ready. Children are only able to control their bladder and bowels when they are **physically** ready and when they **want** to be dry and clean.

Successful toilet training is dependent on a bladder that can hold and then release urine in a flood rather than continual drips. To check readiness observe how long a nappy remains dry, generally the bladder needs to be able to retain urine for over an hour. The child also needs to recognise the sensation of passing urine. Some children will 'stop' or hover, once you can recognise these moments try to establish verbal links to these sensations. 'I think you have had a wee,' consistency of language and terminology across nursery and home is essential.

Some children can feel anxious when they start toilet training at this sensitive and delicate point the consistency of their key person can make a significant difference to their experiences.

In my experience, once children display readiness for toileting, it is best to adopt a simplistic approach. Put them in pants or pull-ups and explain they are going to use the potty/nursery toilet today. As soon as you see the child knows when they are going to wee, encourage them to use their potty.

The building blocks for learning

> **Practice point**
>
> Leave the potty where it can be seen and explain what it is for. Practice sitting on it for a couple of days before starting training. It is usually easier if boys start by sitting on the potty before they switch to standing up later on.

Do not fuss over an accident; young children who do not feel anxious and worried are more likely to be successful the next time. Put them in clothes that are easy to change and avoid tights and clothes with zips or lots of buttons.

It can be quite tricky to get the balance right between giving praise and making a big deal out of it. It is crucial two-year-olds do not feel under pressure as this may affect their ability to relax and recognise the signs.

I would avoid constant reminders; it is vital that children learn to recognise the signs themselves. While constant reminders may prevent accidents, it may also encourage the child to rely on adults rather than accepting the signs.

Remember every child is different.

Sleep times

The key person needs to be observant around two-year-old children's need for sleep as a tired two-year-old can quickly become a distressed two-year-old. Tiredness can have a significant effect on a two-year-old's behaviour, making them more prone to tantrums and other age-related behaviours.

Parents may not be fully aware of the importance of sleep for their young child, getting the balance between the child's need for sleep and parents' wishes can be tricky. Regular communication with parents is essential, negotiating and compromise is often the way forward, allowing children to have a shorter or earlier sleep time can be a way to balance the child's physical requirements alongside parents' wishes.

> **Practice point**
>
> Environments to encourage sleep:
>
> - A calm, quiet place
> - Low-level lighting
> - Sleep mat/bag
> - A cover to pull over

- Comforter if required
- Consistent routine
- Familiar adult

Children can resist the urge to sleep if they are not entirely settled, initially it is vital that the key person maintains proximity to offer the reassurance and sensitive responses required to help the child feel safe and secure. Equally, waking up can also be disorientating; children need their familiar adult who understands their individual needs.

Mealtime

The expectations of sitting with others and feeding themselves can be challenging and potentially a new experience for some two-year-olds. Sitting in small social groups with their key worker make meal times a relaxed and social event.

Meal times can involve long periods of sitting; in my experience, it is best to wait until the meal is ready before you ask children to come and sit down. Involve the children in setting the table, having individual place mats helps organise the seating arrangements and provides children with their own boundary.

Encouraging two-year-old's independence in serving their food and pouring the drinks provides opportunities for children to make choices about the portion size.

It is important to avoid stressful meal times, do not overreact if children seem uninterested in their food, young children do respond to gentle, positive encouragement and a playful approach, they are also more inclined to eat and try new foods if they see others eating.

Children quickly pick up on attitudes to food; it is crucial that adult's role model good eating habits, sitting and eating meals with children in the nursery will build positive habits.

Point for action

An effective key person approach has to become part of the nursery philosophy and a central focus of all daily routines.

Routines

In the day-to-day workings of a busy nursery, the key person approach can become diluted. The pressure to get through the bathroom and mealtime routines can put stress on the key person approaches. It is essential that these issues are worked through and a clear understanding of the importance of these care activities established.

> **Pause for thought**
>
> Daily routines for two-year-olds.
>
> How effective is the key worker role during daily routines?
>
> What works well?
>
> What can you do differently?
>
> How could you improve young children's experiences?

Building and maintaining a key person approach based on the effective principles and values of working with two-year-old children will be both complex and challenging. The key person approach is more than a rota or schedule of work, it is an approach that is motivated and driven by practitioners and staff who understand how important it is to get it right for young children.

Young children only get one chance at childhood; it is essential that we get it right. Making time to read and reflect on research and developmental theory is essential. Questioning and discussing how the key worker approach fits within nursery routines and practices is a necessity and the responsibility of all who work with young children.

Elfer et al. (2003) suggest part of the key person approach is the process of working and struggling together to:

- Hear everyone's point of view
- Help each other develop ideas and possibilities
- Put proposals into practice and try them out
- Build on what seems to work and to find another way when something does not

Future challenge

The activity can be completed individually or as a team activity. The activity aims to develop discussion and sharing of ideas and understanding around the *implementation of the key person approach* in nurseries working with two-year-old children and their families.

Using a theoretical reflective cycle or develop your own model take some time to consider; **the effectiveness of your key worker approach.**

The following questions may help to guide your reflection:

How does the key person approach translate into practice?

What works well?

What are the challenges?

What have you gained from this activity? Share your thoughts and ideas with colleagues.

PART 3
The environment for learning
Provision and practice

8 Playing and learning

What does learning through play actually mean and what is the adult role?

Two-year-old children thrive when they can be active agents in their own learning. Through the process of play young children are able to construct ideas and thoughts about the world, they develop a belief in themselves, confidence to experiment and try things out – young children learn how to learn.

It is well documented that early experiences have lasting repercussions on a child's social, emotional, physical and cognitive development. Early learning impacts on a child's whole life; their experiences and learning in school and how successful and fulfilled they become as adults.

Enabling all children to reach their full potential is an aspiration commonly stated in early childhood policies. If this is to be achieved, we must first understand *how* young children learn. This chapter will explore and unpick the characteristics of effective learning. Unravelling what learning through play actually means and providing guidance on the role of the adult in supporting two-year-old children's play.

Pedagogy

When people talk about the pedagogy of teaching they are referring to the way practitioners meet young children's needs. The environment, resources and activities we provide for young children are based on our pedagogical principles.

The environment for learning

> **Point of note**
>
> Pedagogy is defined simply as the method and practice of teaching. It encompasses teaching styles, feedback and assessment and teacher theory.

When planning an activity, we will consider the child's age, interest and developmental stage – these considerations reflect our knowledge and belief about the child and how the child learns. The justifications behind these decisions form our pedagogical principles.

Reflecting on our practice, asking questions about:

- What we do
- Why we do it
- Its impact on young children's learning

Leads us to learn more about our practice and ourselves; we begin to establish our pedagogical practices with young children. It takes time to develop our pedagogical principles.

> **Pause for thought**
>
> Consider your work with two-year-old children.
>
> What are your pedagogical principles?
>
> What influences your pedagogy?
>
> How have your pedagogical principles changed?

Knowledge of child development, the importance of establishing strong relationships with young children and their families, the role of the key person, the importance of providing suitable environments form part of our pedagogical principles.

Although every child is unique, all young children share the same learning characteristics. Knowing *how* two-year-old children learn provides the confidence to make decisions around provision practice and adult roles and how to adjust practice and provision to meet the specific needs of individual children in the setting.

Describing *how* children learn Dame Clare Tickell, in her review on the Early Years Foundation Stage (2011: 27), highlighted the three characteristics of effective teaching and learning as; playing and exploring, active learning and creative and thinking critically.

While in reality children do not make distinctions in their learning and each strand of the characteristics of effective teaching and learning are intrinsically woven; for the purpose of this discussion, each strand will be explored and discussed separately.

> **Pause for thought**
>
> Are you familiar with the characteristics of effective play?
>
> What are the characteristics of effective play?
>
> What do they mean to you?
>
> How do they impact/influence you?

Playing and exploring – engagement

The phrase learning through play is frequently repeated in the early years, yet precisely *how* play relates to learning is a little less clear for many who work with young children.

Play is an elusive and complex concept to define, there are many forms of play; construction play, role play, rough and tumble play, are only a few. Through play children can work things out, to experiment, imagine, to problem solve, to find alternative ways of doing things, to experience.

The environment for learning

Table 8.1 The learning characteristics represent processes rather than outcomes. (Adapted from Tickell 2011)

Characteristics of learning are:

Playing and exploring: Engagement	–Finding out and exploring –Using what they know in their play –Being willing to have a go
Active learning: Motivation	–Being involved and concentrating –Keep on trying –Enjoying achieving what they set out to do
Creating and thinking critically: Thinking	–Having their own ideas –Using what they already know to learn new things –Choosing ways to do things and find new ways

Abstract thinking. Playing helps young children to work out what they think and feel.

Children learn in many ways, the DCSF (2009) publication highlights the key ways young children learn:

Playing – indoors and out, alone and with others, quietly or boisterously – allows children to find out about things, try out and practise ideas and skills, take risks, explore their feelings, learn from mistakes, be in control and think imaginatively. Playing is an important centre of learning for young children.

Being with other people – as well as developing emotional security and social skills, being with other people – other children and adults – stimulates ideas and involvement that move learning forward.

Being active – young children need to move, and learn and remember things by taking experiences in through the senses as they move. Sitting still for too long can disrupt learning.

Exploring new things and experiences – children's deep curiosity leads them to use all their senses to explore in real hands-on activities, and then put the information together in their own minds to form ideas and make sense of the world.

Talking to themselves – in 'self-speech' children use out-loud thinking to clarify their thoughts, regulate their activities, take on imaginative roles and rehearse their skills.

Communicating about what they are doing with someone who responds to their ideas – even before they can talk in words, children are keen to share their thoughts through sounds, gesture and body language. Talk helps children to understand what they experience. It is crucial that they have a chance to express their own ideas, as well as have conversations to hear other people's ideas, extend their thinking, and use language about learning.

Representing ideas and experiences – children deepen their understanding as they recreate experiences or communicate their thinking in many different ways – in role-play or small world play, pictures, movements, models, and talk.

Meeting physical and mental challenges – working out what to do, trying hard, persevering with problems, finding out and thinking for themselves are opportunities for developing a real understanding. These challenges may occur in the play, or in real-life or planned activities.

Being shown how to do things – children learn skills by watching others or being taught how to do something. Adults or peers may directly instruct, model, guide or demonstrate.

Practising, repeating, applying skills – rehearsing skills in similar tasks or new contexts helps children to build mastery, to enjoy their own expertise, and to consolidate what they can do.

Having fun – there is no place for dull, repetitive activities. Laughter, fun, and enjoyment, sometimes being whimsical and nonsensical, are the best contexts for learning. Activities can be playful even when they are not actually play.

Source: Learning, playing and interacting; Good practice in the Early Years Foundation Stage. DCSF (2009: 9)

Interestingly Tina Bruce, a highly respected academic, theorises that children do not learn *through* play but use play to practice what they have learnt. While the role and function of play continue to be debated, it is acknowledged that high-quality play experience ensures young children's holistic development.

Adults are responsible for developing an indoor and outdoor environment to support two-year-old children's play and exploration. Consideration of how this can be done is further explored in the following chapter.

Tina Bruce identifies 12 features of play:

1. Children use the first-hand experience from life.
2. Children make up rules as they play in order to keep control.
3. Children symbolically represent as they play making props and adapting play props.
4. Children choose to play – they cannot be made to play.

The environment for learning

> 5. Children rehearse their future in their role play.
> 6. Children sometimes play alone.
> 7. Children pretend when they play.
> 8. Children play with adults and other children cooperatively in pairs or groups.
> 9. Children have a personal play agenda, which may or may not be shared.
> 10. Children are deeply involved and difficult to distract from their deep learning as they wallow in their play and learning.
> 11. Children try out their most recently acquired skills and competencies as if celebrating what they know.
> 12. Children coordinate ideas and feelings and make sense of relationships with their families friends and cultures.
>
> Bruce, T (2011) *Learning Through Play: For Babies, Toddlers and Young Children*

As young children's play progresses, it is important to consider the adult role in supporting the play. Knowing when and how to interact with young children's self-initiated play can be difficult. It is important to take time to tune in and find out about the play. Consider your role in the play, is it to become a player, to model techniques or language, or to introduce new concepts and resources.

It is essential not to take over the play, or to direct the play. Two-year-old children will often actively recruit you to play, when they want you there, in contrast, they will also make it quite clear if they do not want you to be part of their play.

Observation

Excited that Emily was at the blackboard mark making, I began to narrate the actions she was making with the paint brush and bucket of water.

'Emily making marks ... big shapes ... curved shapes ... Emily tipping the water ... is the water falling?'

Emily smiled at me and said 'Cover, I cover ... all gone all gone.'

Turning her back on me Emily continued her pursuits of enveloping and covering the board. I took this as Emily signalling that she wished to be left alone.

Discussion
Initially, Emily patiently and politely accepted my attempts at narrating her actions. However, in my haste and excitement, I misinterpreted Emily's actions; it is very evident on this occasion that Emily has both control and

> an understanding of the situation. Emily's body language stated my presence was not required, that she is both competent and capable of continuing without my interference.

Pause for thought

There are times when children need to be free to explore without adult involvement.

How do you always gain permission to join young children in their play pursuits?

It is important not to rush our interpretations of what we believe underpins young children's actions because sometimes we can get it wrong and perhaps it is essential to be aware that a little knowledge may be a hindrance rather than a help (Brierley and Nutbrow 2018: 144).

Active learning – motivation

Being an active participant comes naturally to two-year-old children, their innate curiosity to explore and discover provides intrinsic motivation for learning.

Ferre Laevers proposes learning only occurs when the intensity of attention and involvement in a task are high. Suggesting young children's high levels of involvement can be observed when they are engrossed in their actions; when intrinsic interest and motivation provide the exploratory drive to seek further clarification, the urge to figure it out.

High-level involvement is compared to the concept of 'flow' developed by Csikszentmihalyi (2000). During the state of 'flow' the child becomes lost in the process, experiencing deep levels of concentration and enjoyment.

Providing safe but challenging play opportunities both indoors and outdoors is essential. Providing a balance of familiar activities that allow for consolidation of skills and knowledge alongside new experiences to extend and challenge.

Recognising and praising young children's learning dispositions, praising their resilience, their ability to have another go or find a different way encourages young children to take a risk with their play and persistence in the face of challenge.

Two-year-old children need the time and freedom to become deeply involved in their play. Allow two-year-old children to make their own choices,

The environment for learning

to follow their own interests without adult interference or interruptions for needless housekeeping routines.

> **Pause for thought**
>
> Consider how it feels to be involved.
>
> Have you ever felt in a state of flow? What did it feel like?
>
> Do you observe young children in states of flow?
>
> How would you respond to children who appear to be in a state of flow?

Creating and thinking critically

Definitions of creativity are not straightforward. However, most agree that the creative process involves several components, most commonly:

- Imagination.
- Originality (the ability to come up with ideas and products that are new and unusual).
- Productivity (the ability to generate a variety of different ideas through divergent thinking).
- Problem-solving (application of knowledge and imagination to a given situation).
- The ability to produce an outcome of value and worth.

> **Point of note**
>
> Although creativity is often associated with 'creative' subjects, such as art and music, creativity is not subject specific. Creativity is a way of approaching problem-solving.

Fundamental to the creative environment is the encouragement of children's play. During episodes of play young children naturally use imagination, insight, problem solving, divergent thinking. Providing environments to support creative and critical thinking include many of the aspects already acknowledged; choice, control the opportunity to become immersed to wallow in experiences. Fostering young children's creativity involves creating a supportive emotional environment. Creative thinking requires young children to not only feel safe and secure but valued and respected.

Accepting two-year-old children as capable beings able to actively create and construct, thoughts and ideas require a pedagogy that supports and facilitates young children as 'co-constructor of knowledge' (Janzen 2008: 291).

Ken Robinson has spoken around the world on the subject of creativity, his 2007 TED Talk 'Do Schools Kills creativity' is the most viewed TED talk of all times.

The bad news is he highlights that by the time children leave school they are much less creative than when they started. Somehow children's ability to think creatively is reduced by the process of education. Leading to the question of whether a loss in creativity is a natural consequence of maturing or children feeling constrained by social conventions?

Creativity is nurtured in environments that do not rush the process of coming to know. Environments that allow children and adults to learn together and from each other, environments where there are no right or wrong answers, environments that value all points of view.

In the second year of life children's understanding of spoken language develops rapidly, making it important to model the language of thinking and learning.

Modelling being a learner allows you to share your thinking out loud, talking about your thinking, highlighting awareness of your thoughts your curiosity, puzzlement and wonder. Making your thinking visible.

> ***Creativity*** *is the process of having original ideas that have value.*
> ***Divergent thinking*** *is a thought process or method used to generate creative ideas by exploring many possible solutions.*
> ***Metacognition*** *is thinking about thinking, being aware of our thoughts.*

The environment for learning

> **Pause for thought**
>
> Modelling the language of thinking.
>
> How do you make your thinking visible?
>
> How do you encourage young children to share their thoughts?
>
> How do you encourage young children to think about their thoughts?

Providing for creative thinking requires adults to:
Become a sensitive conversation partner.
Praise and recognise the process.
Use lots of open-ended questions to expand young children's thinking.

- What should we do next?
- Tell me about your ...
- What might happen if?

Encourage divergent thinking – how else can we do this?
    Encouraging inventiveness and different ways to do things.
    Encouraging metacognition – what do you think?
    Young children naturally make sense of their experiences, repeating actions over and over helps them to build understanding, construct ideas and thoughts about how something works. Future practice needs to ensure these skills are both recognised and valued, young children MUST not feel obliged to conform or constrain their creativity.

Playing and learning

Future challenge

The activity can be completed individually or as a team activity. The activity aims to develop discussion and sharing of ideas and understanding of the characteristics of effective learning displayed by two-year-old children.

Using a theoretical reflective cycle or develop your own model take some time to consider; **how play supports two-year-old children learning.**

The following questions may help to guide your reflection.

How does the learning environment provide young children with opportunities too?

Why are play and exploration important?

How can we facilitate two-year-old children's play and exploration?

Why is active learning important?

How can we facilitate two-year-old children as agents of active learning?

Why is critical and creative thinking important?

How can we facilitate two-year-old children's creative and critical thinking?

What have you gained from this activity? Share your thoughts and ideas with colleagues.

9 Schema

Have you ever wondered why young children are so fascinated with filling containers, covering objects in sticky tape, emptying boxes, and pushing around an empty pram? These unusual patterns of behaviour are called schemas.

Knowledge of schema provides an opportunity to feed an inquisitive mind, to nourish curiosity, and provide an environment to extend a young child's thinking. Schematic learning theory is complex; it is not possible within a single chapter to cover all aspects of schema theory.

This chapter intends to build awareness and introduce the notion of schema theory. **Recognising, noticing** and **responding** to young children's schema forms the first steps to:

- Enriching practitioner interactions.
- Nurturing two-year-old children's thinking.
- Provide inspiring environments.
- Empower two-year-old children to construct their own knowledge and understanding of the world.

> ### Practice points
>
> *Noticing, recognising* and ***responding*** *to the intrinsically motivated repeatable actions of two-year-old children at play, allows practitioners and parents to question and critique how the experiences and environments young children inhabit impact their cognitive development.*

The environment for learning

Young children's seemingly random use of resources can be a little perplexing and challenging to comprehend. Using a schematic lens to view young children's actions provides a framework for understanding.

At its simplest level schemas are repetitive actions and patterns in young children's play. Two-year-old children have an insufficient language to explain why they do something. Their exploration is driven by a natural curiosity repeating an action over and over helps a young child develop ideas about how the world works.

Defining schema, Athey (2007: 5) describes a 'pattern of repeatable actions' that lead children's behaviours and thinking. Athey suggests the need to look deeper to look below the surface of the play, to recognise the actions and motivation displayed by the young child.

Figure 9.1 Examples of schematic play

Figure 9.1 (Continued)

The environment for learning

Figure 9.1 (Continued)

Observation: Playdough: 'hiding'.

Abby is not using the play dough to make shapes, but instead pushing the metal shape templates into the play dough; she covers the metal shape templates in play dough.

To push the metal shape templates into the centre of the playdough required such force that she had to use both hands and stand on her tiptoes. Abby continues with this endeavour until the metal templates are entirely covered in dough and have disappeared from view.

Changing her focus Abby placed small pieces of play dough into the palm of her hand. Closing her hand, the playdough disappeared from her view. She repeated this many times. Opening her hand the play dough re-appeared; making Abby smile.

Abby places small pieces of play dough inside other resources, once again she can make the play dough disappeared from view.

> **Discussion**
>
> At 24 months of age it can be assumed that Abby's interest is not in the permanence of the objects, but the actions of enclosing and containing. Abby is interested in **covering** and **enveloping** objects.
>
> Abby explores different ways to make the object disappear from view.
>
> - Using the play dough to cover the metal templates.
> - Using the palm of her hand to hide the play dough.
> - Placing play dough inside resources removes it from her view.
>
> Suggesting Abby's form of thought is **containing** and **enveloping.**

In the observation, Abby's persistent form of thought is about covering and enveloping objects to make them disappear from view. Abby is purposefully exploring her ideas and thoughts through her interactions with the play dough. The malleable properties of play dough facilitate the differing exploration of containing and enveloping allow Abby to nourish her form of thought as she continues to explore and investigate with the play dough.

There are many ways to respond to Abby's interest, playing hide and seek, making dens, planning a treasure hunt, helping with the washing up, putting the clothes in the washing machine, putting things in bags and boxes finding out about the inside of fruit are some of the endless examples of day to day activities involving containing and enveloping.

As adults we view young children's play through the adult eye and adult thinking, adopting a schematic lens to view young children's play provides alternative explanations and theory.

Viewing young children's actions through a schematic lens suggest collecting, lining up, stacking, connecting, hiding and transferring, are actions intrinsically motivated and repeated as part of a two-year-old child's quest to learn about the world they live in.

> **Pause for thought**
>
> Look more closely at young children's fascinations.
>
> What can you learn?
>
> Have you ever underestimated young children's capabilities?

The environment for learning

The power of schema

Schemas sensitise young children to specific elements within the environment. A schematic interest affords young children the ability to recognise meaningful objects in the environment. The two-year-old child becomes skilled in identifying resources and objects that fit their 'threads of thoughts', their interests and fascinations.

Consider the small construction area, children who regularly show an interest in this area is noted using the bricks in different ways:

- George likes to collect the bricks and place them in the basket.
- John enjoys building the bricks into a tall tower.
- Katie loves to create tracks with the bricks and then disconnect it and rebuild it.
- Paul enjoys putting the bricks in a bag and carrying them around.

Each child is exploring different abstract ideas and concept:

- George's interest is to cover and envelope.
- John's fascination involves vertical trajectories.
- Katie's passion involves connecting and separating.
- Paul's preferences include enveloping and transporting.

Pause for thought

Recognise when children display deep levels of involvement.

What actions are they repeating?

What appears to be the form of thought?

Can you recognise links to previous actions?

Does there seem to be continuity, a persistent form of thought?

Schemas can be considered as the perceptions and thoughts young children develop as they make sense of their experiences. Young children demonstrate 'threads of thought' within their thinking, applying these persistent ideas to various activities helps to build an understanding of abstract concepts (Nutbrown 2011). Young children use schematic threads to explore the environment and develop cognitive understanding.

Graphical representation

As young children grow they naturally develop the ability to gain a more sophisticated understanding of the world. Initially, young children gain information through their senses over time and as a result of experience start to achieve a more sophisticated understanding of the world.

Young children's schematic threads help them to fit ideas together to accommodate new understanding and develop more complex cognitive knowledge. Recognising a two-year-olds schema requires the appreciation that young children's thinking can be also be expressed graphically. Paying attention to young children's mark making can provide many clues to the complexity of their thinking – young children use mark making as a form of graphically representing their thoughts.

> **Point for practice**
>
> *Learning about schema provides a way to understand and support young children's cognitive development.*

Research and evidence of two-year-olds use of figurative schemas are limited (Brierley 2018), but recent study is starting to support two-year-old children's use of mark making to represent their emergent thoughts. Suggesting the drawing and paintings produced by two-year-old children represent their thoughts and perceptions gained through the actions of twirling, running, jumping up and down and messing around with objects.

Recognising schemas in young children's patterns of play helps to make the learning visible, affording adults the opportunities to **notice** and gain understanding. With understanding comes the ability to **respond**, the ability to facilitate and extend young children's learning.

The environment for learning

> **Observation: Graphical representation**
>
> *Over a period of time, Abby has explored her interest in a vertical trajectory schema.*
>
> - *At home in the garden on the slide, swing and trampoline.*
> - *In nursery tipping and pouring water.*
>
> *These experiences have provided Abby with both the physical experience and visual perception of a vertical trajectory movement.*
>
> *The information Abby gains from her encounters with the environment is fitted and accommodated within her schema, her cognitive understanding (Athey 2007). As young children develop and grow their ability to think and understand becomes more complex. Abby's cognitive theories and knowledge of vertical trajectories are becoming more complex.*
>
> *Abby is regularly observed using a paintbrush and water to make downward vertical marks on the wall suggesting Abby can replay the movement patterns in her mind and represent them as figurative marks.*

Pause for thought

Graphically representing thoughts.

What access to mark making do children regularly have?

How do children demonstrate connections between their physical movements and their mark making?

Table 9.1 Popular schemas to identify

Recognise	Notice	Respond
Transporting schema is characterised by transporting objects from one place to another.	A child carrying bricks from one place to another in a bag or box. Pushing a friend around in a pram or truck. Moving sand from indoors to outdoors. General moving objects to the 'wrong place'.	Allowing and supporting the movement of resources around the room and from indoor to outdoors. Providing boxes, bags, trucks and prams to transport resources in.

(*Continued*)

Table 9.1 (Cont.)

Recognise	Notice	Respond
Trajectory (vertical or horizontal) schema is a fascination with straight lines and the dynamic movement of objects through space.	Climb up and jump off furniture, play with running water at the tap, bounce and kick balls. Ride bikes and scooters, enjoy running.	Ball games, dancing, paper planes bubble blowing, providing running water. Supporting children to make climbing and balancing frames from crates and planks.
Enclosing and enveloping Enclosing schema is about enclosing objects or oneself within a boundary, building enclosures and putting thing within the enclosure.	Sitting in the sand tray and covering their legs with sand. Getting face covered with food at lunchtime, getting covered in water when playing at the water tray. Wrapping dolls in blankets. Painting over pictures.	Den making, dressing up. Using water and brushes to paint (cover) floor and walls. Using paint, shaving foam to cover objects. Looking inside fruit and vegetables.
Ordering and positioning schema is characterised by the static element of ordering or lining up objects and toys to explore positions and space.	A child may put things on their head, order objects in a specific way. Becoming upset if their food on the plate touches. Enjoy sitting under the table.	Provide plenty of small resources for ordering and lining up. Acknowledging meal times are also learning opportunities, use language to support schematic interest your carrots are 'next' to the meat.
Containing schema is the fascination of placing things inside things, often associated with an interest in insideness.	Filling and emptying containers of all kinds. Putting objects inside other objects. Climbing into boxes small spaces, being contained.	Support opportunities to explore the insideness of objects. Provide resources of differing weight and texture to be contained.

Schema spotting

Recognising and **noticing** the schematic interests displayed in young children's play is compared by Nutbrown (2011: 46) with 'unlocking a door, shining a light on previously darkened areas, seeing a new'. Schema provides a lens and opportunity, to gain insight and understanding of how two-year-old children build their ideas, concepts and knowledge of the world.

Responding and nurturing schematic interests' progresses the formation of young children's cognitive structures, their thinking and learning.

The environment for learning

Starting with schema

Reading about schemas provides ideas of what to look for, the next step is to recognise and note this behaviour in children's play.

> **Point of note**
>
> Heuristic play was initially developed by Eleanor Goldschmeid.
> Heuristic play is a planned and organised session delivered across the nursery day.
> It is an approach that offers young children the opportunity to play freely without adult intervention. Young children are provided with a large number of various resources and object to explore.

Heuristic play provides real opportunities for young children to discover their threads of thinking and explore the concepts and ideas they have formulated.

Heuristic play provides the opportunity to explore objects and find out 'what they can do'.

Once emotionally comfortable and confident, young children quickly become engrossed and involved in their exploration of the objects.

Young children will:

- Fill and empty
- Sort objects
- Form collections
- Drop objects
- Fit together and disconnect
- Place inside/on top/behind/
- Cover object Stack and pile
- Pour and tip from containers (it can be noisy)

Heuristic play provides endless opportunities for satisfying and promoting schematic threads of thought.

The session should ideally last an hour with no disruptions. A clear defined space is required. Set out the resources before the start of the session, engage the children with the tidying away at the end of the session.

Schema

Heuristic play sessions

The adult role:

- To sit close, offering emotional security and reassurance.
- Giving facial and bodily movement to indicate their presence and care.
- It is fundamentally a non-social activity – the young child is gaining pleasure and satisfaction from investigating the objects.
- To observe, to learn more about the child.
- To ensure safety.

What to expect

- Pick up objects, move them about
- Put objects in containers
- Take objects out of containers
- Pile up objects/knock them down
- Roll objects
- Slide objects
- Slot small into larger
- Shake and bang
- Line up objects
- Put rings on rods, posts etc.
- Spin round/cylindrical objects
- Drop objects from a height
- Screw and unscrew lids
- Looking inside or through objects
- Squeeze objects
- Drape ribbons, chains etc. around self/furniture
- Hide objects in new places
- Collect similar or same objects

Suggested materials

- Natural objects- pine cones, pebbles, shells
- Household objects – metal and wooden spoons, plugs pastry brushes, keys
- Recycled objects- spools, bubble wrap, crisp tubes card roles
- Toys – wooden blocks ping pong balls, stacking cubes, boxes
- General purpose object – plugs chains door handles
- It is advised to have a minimum of 50 objects

Heuristic play is an ideal time for practitioners to observe children's actions and explorations; a time to **recognise** and **notice** individual children's schematic interests.

The environment for learning

- To make connections between children's present experiences and previous experiences.
- To note the continuity of actions from one day to the next.
- To recognise the cognitive connections between seemingly different activities.

Responding to schematic interest extends a young child's thinking and learning.

- To respond with appropriate language and conversations to help young children link ideas.
- To support children to revisit experiences and develop more complex levels of understanding.

Schema theory highlights the concepts and ideas that interest young children, to value the matches made between thought and environmental content as young children actively construct their own knowledge and ideas about the environments they inhabit.

The environment must extend young children's thinking and learning supporting the threads of children's thinking across time.

> **Pause for thought**
>
> The environment.
>
> How open-ended are the materials?
>
> How do the resources available allow children to personalise their explorations?

Recognising schematic patterns permits a deeper understanding of *how* two-year-old children learn. Knowledge of schema enables tuning in to children's forms of thinking, to match language and resources to support young children's learning and thinking further. Schema theory helps to foreground the connections and continuity in young children's thinking.

Schema

> **Point for action**
>
> *Sharing and discussing observations of young children's play with colleagues can form an essential part of your continuing professional development and enhance the learning experiences of young children.*

The following chapter will consider how schematic threads of thought can form the basis for developing provision and learning environments for two-year-old children.

> **Future challenge**
>
> The activity can be completed individually or as a team activity. The activity aims to develop discussion and sharing of ideas and understanding of using schema to gain a deeper understanding of how two-year-old children learn.
>
> Using a theoretical reflective cycle or develop your own model take some time to consider; the role of schema in two-year-old children's learning.
>
> The following questions may help to guide your reflection.
>
> *What is schema?*
>
> *Why is schema theory important for those who work with two-year-old children?*
>
> *How can knowledge of schema influence pedagogical practice with two-year-old children?*
>
> *How is schema theory shared with parents?*
>
> *Why is schema theory shared with parents?*
>
> What have you gained from this activity? Share your thoughts and ideas with colleagues.

10 The learning environment

Young children thrive and develop when they have access to stimulating indoor and outdoor environments. Providing environments to support two-year-old's play, requires a considerable amount of thought and planning. Two-year-old children play very differently from three-year-olds meaning some of the traditional ideas around how nursery environments are set out are a little redundant.

Two-year-old children are akin to explorers, they spend their days investigating how things work, continually formulating ideas, to try and test out. Supporting and encouraging this natural curiosity in young children requires an environment with 'open-ended' resources; resources with no limits (Brierley and Nutbrow 2018).

Young children need to be outdoors as much as indoors, they need extended periods of play in environments that challenge and allow risk-taking, environments that are dynamic, flexible and full of irresistible stimulus.

The environment and the resources we provide for two-year-old children must support inclusion and reflect age appropriate needs, to do this we must consider how two-year-old plays.

> **Points for practice**
>
> *Open-ended resources include:*
> *Commercial materials – blocks, Duplo, small world – people, cars animals and fantasy figures*
> *Collections of natural materials – stick, stones, shells, pebbles, sand and water*
> *Malleable materials – play dough, gloop, flubber, dough*
> *Recycled materials – cardboard boxes, tubes, sheets, planks, crates*

The environment for learning

Age appropriateness

The previous chapter explored the concept of schema identifying some of the repeated patterns of actions that can be recognised in two-year-old children's play. These repeated patterns can be used as a basis from which to plan, organise and resource effective indoor and outdoor environments for two-year-old children. It is essential to consider how the outdoor environment can be organised and resources to compliments and extend the indoor provision.

Earlier chapters highlighted the importance of two-year-old's physicality, the importance of whole body movement their incessant need to move, their embodied approach to learning. Meaning consideration of space is an important and vital aspect when planning and designing the environment for two-year-olds.

> **Pause for thought**
>
> Consider the layout and organization of the learning environment provided for your two-year-old children.
>
> What works well?
>
> What do your children enjoy doing?
>
> What difficulties do you experience?

Revisiting some of the popular patterns of actions displayed naturally by two-year-olds during free play provides ideas and structure for developing and planning two-year-old provision. Reflecting on young children's actions and uses of resources offers essential insights for resources in supporting young children's holistic learning.

Bodily movement

Two-year-olds like to experience the physicality of their bodily movement, running, jumping and crawling are all described as intrinsically motivated movements and actions.

The learning environment

Figure 10.1 Intrinsically motivated movement

Athey's (2007) work confirms the links between a child's motor actions and sensory feedback as central to the learning process. Behaviour's that may on the surface seem to be pointless and even disrupted are in fact an example of embodied learning. Running, jumping and crawling are all examples of two-year-olds using their kinaesthetic sense (the feeling of movement) to support their learning.

Providing space indoors and outdoors to allow and actively encourage bodily movement is vital for two-year-old play. It may not be possible to have all types of movement opportunities available at the same time, in this case, consider how the movement opportunities vary across the day and week.

Resources and ideas

Low climbing and jumping activities, allows children to gain the sensation of height in a controlled environment both indoors and outdoors.

The environment for learning

Provide open space for exploring large body movements, space to twirl, to crawl, to lie flat on the floor.

Adult-led activity – hide and seek – ring games – action songs – obstacle courses provide further reassurance and security for less confident children, it also offers opportunities to model techniques and reinforces the suitable language.

* Risk assessments will need to be completed to ensure there are no additional dangers or risks; all resources are stable and not going to overbalance or tip.

Transporting

Moving things from one place to another is a popular pass time for many two-year-olds. Young children who like to transport objects from place to place will use a variety of means to move the object, including bags, boxes, trucks and prams. Once transported the objects may simply be tipped out and left.

Figure 10.2 Transported spoons and containers

The learning environment

It is essential to consider how we organise large resources as transporters will explore the transportation of sensory materials; transporting the sand into the water and vice versa. Providing containers and shelves around the sand and water area can provide more suitable places to transport the materials to.

Resources and ideas

Equipment to aid transporters will include a plentiful source of differing size and weighted objects alongside a varied range of transportation options varying from bags to carry, or pushchairs and trucks to push and pull.

Providing empty containers placed strategically around the indoor and outdoor environment can offer destinations for the transported objects.

Be aware young children will make no distinction between transporting objects indoors and outdoors, meaning some resources can get left outside in differing weather conditions.

Figure 10.3 Transporting friends

The environment for learning

Tipping, throwing and scattering

Two-year-olds can become fascinated with the dynamic movement of objects exploring these fascinations could involve throwing, tipping and scattering objects.

Young children who throw, tip or scatter are exploring the sensory feedback gained from these activities. Throwing, tipping or scattering objects provide an embodied feeling of satisfaction, watching its trajectory through the air, the distance it travels, the sound it makes as it hits the floor, all provide sensory feedback to the young child.

The visual pattern of small jigsaw pieces scattered across the floor, some pieces roll others bounce, how far the bean-bag travels, the pattern and movement of the water as it is tipped onto the floor.

Two-year-olds will use the resources they naturally find in the nursery environment to explore their throwing, tipping and scattering fascinations. This intrinsic curiosity cannot be halted a balance needs to be struck in providing suitable spaces and times for these actions.

Resources and ideas

Provide bean bags, beanie toys or small foam balls to throw, plan activities for target throwing into a hoop a box.

A wide selection of buckets, bowls, trays and jugs to tip water, sand or dry pasta into and from. The large tuff trays provide an enclosed area for containing the scattered objects.

Blow or Splatter painting with water or paint.

Build a tower and offer a controlled opportunity to knock it down.

> **Pause for thought**
>
> The outdoor learning environment.
>
> What does the outdoor environment offer that indoors cannot?
>
> How does your outdoor environment compliment the indoor environment?
>
> How do your outdoor resources provide experiences on a larger scale?

Up and down

Interest in vertical and horizontal trajectories is widespread for young children. Finding piles and lines of seemingly random resources is evidence of a trajectory interest. The stacking ordering and lining up of objects is a typical pass time for many two-year-olds. Young children are fascinated by the size and shapes they can build, spreading the resources takes up more space, squeezing then together creates different spaces.

Some two-year-olds will use their bodies to explore horizontal and trajectory movements, the enjoyment of walking up and down the room, riding the bike, climbing up the slide, coming down the slide.

Two-year-old children will also want to explore how using different body parts changes their perception they feel. Bottom shuffling up the steps, sliding down head first or backwards all provide different sensory experiences.

It is not uncommon for young children to become a little fixed in their choice of resources. Always wanting to go on the bike or the scooter on these occasions it is essential to ensure the environment offers other opportunities to gain similar sensory feedback.

Resources and ideas

Young children will use an array of nursery resources to explore the concepts of stacking, ordering and lining. Consider the resources freely available, flat sided objects are easier to stack and order than those with curved sides. Flat surfaces provide less challenge than a slope!

It is crucial to provide a selection of resources and activities to support young children's exploration of their bodily movement. To walk, to hop, to bottom shuffle, to walk forwards to walk backwards all provide different sensory feedback. Travelling across a flat surface, a raised platform, a slope has a different feel.

A selection of wooden logs, tyres, crates and short planks provide untold opportunities for young children to explore different ways to travel.

Young children love to tip and pour water, consider how to extend the use of water in the outdoor environment.

Containing and enveloping

Two-year-old children love placing themselves or objects in confined spaces and containers, covering and wrapping objects, before placing them inside the pram or the play washing machine. Finding the baby doll inside the washing machine is evidence of

The environment for learning

a child exploring their interest with containing. Young children who continually want to wash their hand's links to enveloping and covering their hands with soap and water.

Many young children who on the surface enjoy playing in the home corner, may actually be exploring concepts around containing and enveloping. Filling baking trays with plasticine before placing inside the oven, putting all the cups and plates into the sink.

Dressing the baby before wrapping in a blanket and placing inside the cot. Wearing the dressing up clothes, attempting to climb into the toy cot are expected behaviours demonstrated by young children exploring their enveloping fascination.

Further consideration must be the use of language, using language to narrate and describe the actions displayed by two-year-old children provides opportunities to support learning and language development further.

> **Pause for thought**
>
> Consider young children's language.
>
> What accompanying language do children use during their play activities?
>
> How do you match children's actions with accompanying language?

Resources and ideas

Traditional sand and water areas (indoor and outdoor) provided at the correct height and with suitable access for two-year-olds offers huge opportunities for containing and enveloping explorations.

Shells, beanbags, fir cones, pasta, toy cars, toy people, are a few of the many resources suitable for containing and enveloping.

Playing with shaving foam, gloop, water, play dough flour will promote enveloping opportunities.

Consider the opportunities offered for containing and enveloping the whole body; being within an enclosed space or covering up; some children love wearing wellington boots and a raincoat in all weathers.

Cardboard boxes are ideal for sitting and hiding inside, two-year-olds enjoy squeezing into confined spaces. Being under furniture and inside canopies are all very exciting opportunities for two-year-olds.

Psychological environment

The psychological environment is often described as the hidden curriculum and derived unconsciously as a result of staff beliefs and attitudes. The psychological environment sends strong messages to young children about what is essential and valued. Children can inadvertently learn that particular skills hold higher value or are classed as more important for example the ability to complete a jigsaw over-riding the bike.

Finding out about children's home and cultural experiences are also important if children and families are to feel genuinely included and valued members of the nursery.

Building an effective environment also includes considering how the psychological environment meets young children's social and emotional needs.

Two-year-old children will not benefit from a stimulating environment if their social and emotional needs are not also embraced. Play and learning is dependent on feeling safe and secure, having trust in the people around provides the confidence for two-year-old children to explore the physical environment to build the resilience and strategies to cope with new and challenging situations.

Point of action

The following activity can be completed individually or as a team. The activity aims to develop discussion and sharing of ideas and understanding around developing the learning environment for two-year-old children.

Use the resource audit to:

1. Reflect and identify the types of actions observed in young children's play – discuss key children.
2. Identify possible interest – link to schema play actions.
3. Consider the resources available.
4. Action plan future resource development.

The environment for learning

Table 10.1 Resource audit

Play actions	Possible Interest	Current resources	Action – future resources
Moving objects in truck	Transporting	Bricks Duplo	Increase natural resources – pebbles, pine cones
Carrying objects in bags		Truck Small pram	Selection of bags with different closures – zips, clasp, Velcro
Usually has hands full of stuff		Selection of handbags	Larger sturdy truck
Emptying toys into water tray	Containing		
Dolls in washing machine			
Running up and down	**Trajectory**		
Pushing cars of tables			

Books and storytelling

Sharing and telling stories needs to form part of the daily session with two-year-olds. Sharing books and telling stories provides enormous opportunities for language development, consolidating and introducing new vocabulary, modelling conversations asking and answering questions and time for talk will aid a young child's communication and language development. Feeling secure and having close proximity to the adult ensures a two-year-old can maintain their attention on the story, this means to work effectively, book sharing and storytelling needs to be done on an individual basis or in pairs.

Books that are age appropriate, and have repetition allow young children to join in, but more importantly the young child needs to be interested and excited by the book.

Selecting books with stories to match young children's play actions (schema) can provide a good starting place.

Playspace

The organisation of the environment and its resources needs careful consideration. Two-year-old children's natural preference for playing will be the floor or low tables if play opportunities are placed at regular table height young children will prefer to stand and lean against the table.

Ensure the space is not overcrowded with tables of storage units as this can hinder play opportunities.

Points for practice

From time to time it is helpful to view the environment from the young child's perspective. Kneel in the centre of the room, what can you see, what can you access, where are the difficulties and bottlenecks?

Do not assume commercially purchased products are correct, check water or sand trays are positioned at a height that allows young children to reach to the bottom of the tray.

Books that link to popular actions displayed in young children's play.

Table 10.2

Interest	Title, author
Containing	Time for a bath – Gershator, Phillis
	Spot goes shopping – Hill, Eric
	Five minutes' peace – Murphy, Jill
	Billy's bucket – Gray, Kes
	Whatever next – Murphy, Jill
Enclosing and enveloping	Peep inside range … – Milbourne, Anna
	Spot goes to the farm – Hill, Eric
	Spot goes to the park – Hill, Eric
	Ten in the bed – Dale, Penny
	Peppa's post
Trajectory	We're going on a picnic – Hutchins, Pat
	The blue balloon – Inkpen, Mick
	The runaway pancake – Mackinnon, Mairi
	Red car green car – Walter, Jackie
	Room on the broom – Donaldson, Julia
	A perfect day for it – Fearnley, Jan

(Continued)

Table 10.2 (Cont.)

Interest	Title, author
Transporting	Rusty's train ride – Amery, Heather
	Noisy tractor – Rentta, Sharon
	Walking through the jungle – Lacome, Julie
	Rosie's walk – Hutchins, Pat
	Mr Gumpy's outing – Burningham, John
	Ti tip dig dig – Garcia, Emma
	Pumpkin soup – Cooper, Helen
Rotation	Kipper's birthday – Inkpen, Mick
	The wheels on the bus – Twinn, Anne
	Slow down George – Holwaty, Lauren
	The very busy spider – Carle, Eric

Access to resources

The storage and accessibility of resources can be a challenge, a balancing act between developing independence and maintaining a degree of organisation.

Storage boxes loaded with resources can quickly become cumbersome and awkward for two-year-old children to manipulate when moving from the shelf to the floor. It is often better to have a less is more attitude, allowing more resources to be added to the play as required.

Having smaller quantities of resources available also prevent health and safety hazards occurring when resources become tipped and scattered across the floor.

Independence and inclusion are essential aspects of an effective indoor and outdoor environment, it is important to regularly check young children can reach and have independent access to the resources.

The learning environment

> **Future challenge**
>
> The activity can be completed individually or as a team activity. The activity aims to develop discussion and sharing of ideas and understanding around developing the provision and learning environment to meet the specific needs of two-year-old children.
>
> *Using a theoretical reflective cycle or develop your own model take some time to consider;* **the indoor and outdoor learning environment: extending two-year-old children's play.**
>
> *The following questions may help to guide your reflection.*
>
> - How do you ensure you challenge and stimulate two-year-olds?
> - What materials are freely available?
> - What additional experiences do you provide?
> - How do you support young children's interests and fascinations?
>
> - How do you extend young children's interests and fascinations?
> - What role does language play in supporting two-year-olds play and learning?
>
> **What have you gained from this activity?** Share your thoughts and ideas with colleagues.

Play provides opportunities for learning and social and emotional development; it is crucial for the holistic development of two-year-old children. The true potential of play can only be achieved when we get it right – the environment and the resources we provide for two-year-old children need to be carefully and purposefully chosen. It is crucial we get it right!

> Play not only teaches us how to learn, it is the magic at the heart of childhood and the secret to a satisfying life.
>
> (Hughes 2016: 11)

The documentation process

Evidence of learning

The process of learning and coming to know is complex; young children learn through being physically active, through experiencing real situations, through playing and being with the people who love them. This chapter takes an insightful look at the purpose and practice of recording two-year-old children's learning. Reflecting on the observation process helps those who work and care for young children, to become informed and better able to support the learning and development process.

This chapter aims to explore the idea of pedagogical documentation, a process that allows educators, children and families to learn together while feeding the planning and assessment process. This chapter is about finding purposeful ways to document two-year-old children's achievements.

Why keep records?

The information and records kept on two-year-old children originates mainly from observations, concerns are frequently voiced about the amount of time and paperwork involved in such record keeping. However, the real issue is not about the *amount* of records kept. It is about the *quality* of the records, how effective they are in supporting young children's holistic development.

> **Pause for thought**
>
> Record keeping should be about more than meeting the statutory requirement of any curriculum, consider the records you keep about your children.
>
> Why do you keep records? Who are they for?

The environment for learning

> How do they inform future learning?
>
> What do you gain from them?

The observation process

The observation itself is nothing more than a technique to observe and record information. Observations used to inform responses to young children's needs require more than just seeing and recording, it requires reflection and analysis.

Reflecting on observations provides opportunities to recall the experience, 'think about it, mull it over and evaluate it' (Boud, Keogh and Walker 1985: 43), produce ideas, thoughts and factual explanations to inform and better able practitioners to support the learning and development process. Reflection provides the bridge between what we see and the analysis of our understanding of the child against aspects of development and learning.

Regardless of the different forms of observation, the process remains constant.

Observing – collecting the evidence

Reflection and analysis- what does this mean for the child
Possible links to learning

Implications for future practice & next steps - planning

Observing, analysing, making judgements and deciding what to do next are all part of the observation process. Observations confirm a child's progress and capabilities at a single point in time.

Pedagogical documentation is the collection and organisation of individual observations; building a picture, highlighting and plotting the subtle changes in a young child's development over time. Pedagogical documentation supports a pedagogical approach to assessment.

> **Point of note**
>
> EYFS commitment card 3.1 states:
> Observe children to find out about their needs, what they are interested in and what they can do; note children's responses in different situations; analyse your observations and highlight children's achievements or their need for further support; involve parents as part of the ongoing observation and assessment process.

Parent and child voice

Constructing a holistic picture of a child requires the complementary knowledge of parents and educator. Involving parents in the observation process provides opportunities to develop interpretations and more in-depth understanding of young children's interests and learning.

Talking with parents before or during the 'settling in process', is the start of the observation process. However, maintaining parents' voices in the process is dependent on building strong collaborative and reciprocal relationships.

Involving young children in the observation process is also essential, sharing observation videos and pictures with two-year-old children provides an opportunity to practice their reflective skills: reflect back, to critically think about themselves, experience metacognitive thinking. Sharing observations demonstrate how we valued two-year-olds ideas and thinking it also contributes to the building of self-esteem and wellbeing.

Providing a space for parent and child's voice on observation proformas can ensure we start to *listen*. However, listening is not enough, we need to ensure we *hear* and *respond* to these voices.

The advent of technology allows **pedagogical documentation** to be constructed and stored in many ways. Electronic forms of storage are often seen as convenient, economical and space saving, sending an observation to parents via email may suit busy lifestyles. However, careful thought and consideration need to be taken. Pedagogical documentation is a working document; charting and evidencing an individual child's progress and development over time. It must be easily accessible for children, parents and practitioner to share and enjoy together.

> **Pause for thought**
>
> Consider a recent observation you have completed.
>
> What did it tell you about the child's learning and development?

The environment for learning

> What did you learn from your involvement in the observation process?
>
> How can you share this new knowledge with colleagues and parents?

What and when to observe

Knowing what and when to observe can be confusing; it is the quality and significance of the observation rather than the quantity of observations. Two-year-old children's responses to situations can vary capturing the wholeness and integrity of two-year-old children, requires observations to be made at different times and locations. The consistent factor must be play, capturing the evidence during two-year-old children's freely chosen play activities.

We talk about the quality and significance of the observation, quality and significant moments only occur when two-year-old children become fully immersed and involved in their play.

The Leuven well-being and involvement scales identify how becoming intensely engaged in an activity is considered a necessary condition for deep level learning and development.

Point for practice

Well-being and involvement scales.

Leuven has developed a 5-point scale to measure involvement.

Involvement is being intensely engaged in an activity is considered a necessary condition for deep level learning and development.

The Leuven scale for involvement

Level	Well-being	Signals
1	Extremely low	A young child appears absent, displays little energy in the play, looking around to see what others are doing.
2	Low	Play activity is not continuous; a young child engaged in the activity for only 50% of the time, easily interrupted and distracted by surroundings.
3	Moderate	Mainly continuous play, busy and concentrating but still easily distracted. Concentration is low.

(Continued)

(Cont).		
Level	Well-being	Signals
4	High	Continuous activity; activity has intense moments. They are not easily distracted.
5	Extremely high	Continuous and intense activity; concentrating, creative, energetic and persistent.

Observation chart based on Leuven Involvement Scales for young children (Laevers et al. 1997)

There are many different **types of observations**; being prepared, knowing when and how to use the different observation techniques is important.

Planned or focused observations encourage stepping back from the child. Providing space and time to engage with the observation process fully. When young children are fully involved in their play, a four or five-minute continuous observation will yield a considerable amount of information.

Observations are usually recorded in either written form often referred to as a 'narrative' or through the use of photographs and video clips. Narrative observation is used to record the significant moment in the play, it is crucial not to waste time noting down information that is already known. Instead of focusing on things you do not know – new information.

Recording young children's spoken language can help to provide an understanding of their thinking alongside evidence of their use of language. It is also vital to note non-verbal communication and gesture.

Photographic and video recording are described by Atherton (2013: 30) as 'pauses in action; they hold a moment which has gone but can still be seen'. Photographs and videos provide vast amounts of details and information making it possible to take time to revisit the moment. To look slowly and deeply through the photographs and video to reflect; writing down ideas, thoughts and factual explanations to further accompany the photographs.

Reflecting and analysing the observation requires pondering and deliberating in an attempt to make meaning of the situation. The recognition of what this means

The environment for learning

Focussed or planned observation format

Child name………………………….. Date……………….Location……………..

Activity……………………..

Evidence of involvement

Level	Involvement	Signal

Observation – significant moments

Characteristics of effective learning – underline

Playing and exploring	Active learning	Creating and thinking critically
-Finding out and exploring -Using what they know in their play -Being willing to have a go	-Being involved and concentrating -Keeping on trying -Enjoying achieving what they set out to do	-Having their own ideas -Using what they already know to learn new things -Choosing ways to do things and find new ways

Parents voice Child voice

Reflection analysis

The documentation process

Schemas

Recognise	Notice	Respond

Links to learning
Match to curriculum aspects of learning

Implications for future practice and next steps

for the child and links to possible and future learning can be supported through the use of the observation format example on page.

Tuning into young children's learning and professional development is a very valuable aspect of practice with two-year-old children. Regular involvement with planned and focussed observations provides opportunities for both.

Participant observations involve both participating in the activity and observing simultaneously. Small group activities can provide opportunities to observe young children's personal and social skills, how they interact take turns and respond to

The environment for learning

others. These opportunities cannot always be planned, occurring naturally as part of the working day. It is, for this reason, crucial all staff get in the habit of noting things down or taking photographs as they work.

Incidental observations involve recording significant events that catch your attention as you go about your day-to-day role. Incidental observations often catch young children in action and highlight small but significant events in their life. Having continual access to post it notes or cameras allows these special moments to be recorded and analysed later.

Opportunities for conversations with two-year-old children can frequently happen throughout the day. It is essential to recognise **informal conversations** as part of the observation process. Two-year-old children make no distinctions between activity time and routines, meaning significant moments can happen at any time of the day.

While it may initially feel unnatural talking to two-year-old children about their learning it is important. Initially, this needs to be a conversation about something they have just done or shared a photograph you have just taken. As young children become more familiar with this process and through maturity, they gain a better understanding and ability to reflect on their learning.

Regular use of open-ended questions around learning will elicit young children's reflective skills, encouraging parents to talk about learning with their two-year-old child can also help to highlight the links between play and learning, aiding parents understanding and respect for their young child's play explorations.

Points for practice

It is essential to give young children time to think and respond to questions, don't rush the process. If they seem unable to answer provide a model answer, this may help them to make a connection and better understand the question.

What do you like doing at nursery/at home?
What do you think you learn when you … at nursery/at home?
What do you think you are good at?
What do you find hard to do? How could you get better at this?

International influences

While it is not possible or necessarily desirable to mirror observation approaches from other cultures or practices. Having an understanding and awareness of different cultural values and beliefs can provide further reflective opportunities and the possibility of influencing our own pedagogical ideas and principles.

Based on the Te Whariki curriculum first established by the New Zealand government in 1996. Margret Carr explored the connections between pedagogy and assessment to present the concept of **'learning stories'**. Based around encouraging positive dispositions to learning Carr promotes the use of a narrative enquiry process based around the 4Ds; describing, discussing, documenting and deciding. The publication of her book has founded an increasing interest in this approach.

Loris Malaguzzi is the inspiration behind the **Reggio Emilia** approach. In reaction to his experience of fascism during the war, he wanted to nurture a society of children who could think for themselves. Within the Reggio Emilia schools, learning occurs through the collaboration and dialogue between children, teachers, parents and the community. Project-based on in-depth studies of concepts, ideas, interests and investigations which arise from the children are documented and displayed to illustrate and highlight the children's thoughts, ideas and creativity.

Point of practice

Observing identify and assessing young children's individual learning is exciting and rewarding, but also an essential part of the pedagogical documentation process.

Future challenge

The activity can be completed individually or as a team activity. The activity aims to develop discussion and sharing of ideas and understanding around the recording and documentation of two-year-old children's learning.

Using a theoretical reflective cycle or develop your own model take some time to consider; **the purpose and practice of recording two-year-old children's learning.**

The following questions may help to guide your reflection.

How is time made for observation and reflection process?

The environment for learning

> What is the role of pedagogical documentation?
>
> How children's achievements are shared with other staff?
>
> How the observation process contributes to professional development?
>
> How you share observations are shared with parents and children?
>
> What is the evidence of hearing and responding to parents and child voices?
>
> What have you gained from this activity? Share your thoughts and ideas with colleagues.

Conclusion

As our journey through this book together comes to a close, I would firstly like to take this opportunity to thank you, for taking the time to listen to my ideas, explanations and suggestions.

But crucially I would like to point out that while this journey is coming to an end, this should not be the end. If my years of studying have taught me anything it is the more you learn, the less you know, our journey of discovery must continue.

We must continue to make visible the capabilities of two-year-old children.

We must continue to embody reflection as a professional development tool.

Finally, I would like to close by setting a final *challenge for the future.*

To ensure reflective thinking becomes part of your everyday practice.

To reflect with colleagues, to listen and be open to different perspectives and views every day of your life.

References

Abbott, L. and Langston, A. (eds) (2005) *Birth to Three Matters: Supporting the Framework of Effective Practice*. Maidenhead: McGraw-Hill Education.

Ainsworth, M., Blehar, M., Waters, E. and Wall, S. (1978) *Patterns of Attachment: Assessed in the Strange Situation and at Home*. New Jersey: Erlbaum.

Atherton, F. (2013) *Understanding Schemas and Young Children from Birth to Three*. London: Sage.

Athey, C. (2007) *Extending Thought in Young Children: A Parent-Teacher Partnership*. 2nd ed. London: Paul Chapman Publishing.

Boud, D., Keogh, R. and Walker, D. (1985) *Reflection: Turning Experience into Learning*. London: Routledge.

Bowlby, J. (1988) *A Secure Base: Clinical Application of Attachment Theory*. London: Routledge.

Brierley, J. (2018) Are We Underestimating 2-Year-olds? Recognising the Links between Schema and Mark Making, Implications for Future Pedagogy. *Journal of Early Childhood Research*. 16(2), 136–147.

Brierley, J. and Nutbrow, C. (2018) *Understanding Schematic Learning at Two*. London: Bloomsbury.

Bronfenbrenner, E. (1979) *The Ecology of Human Development: Experiments by Nature and Design*. Cambridge, MA: Harvard University Press.

Bruce, T. (2011) *Learning through Play: For Babies, Toddlers and Young Children*. London: Hodder Education.

Carr, M. and Wendy, L. (2012) *Learning Stories: Constructing Learner Identities in Early Education*. London: Sage.

Claxton, G. and Carr, M. (2004) A Framework for Teaching Learning: The Dynamics of Disposition. *Early Years*. 24(1), 87–97.

References

Csikszentmihalyi, M. (2000) *Beyond Boredom and Anxiety Experiencing Flow in Work and Play*. San Francisco, CA: Jossey-Bass.

DCSF. (2007) *Principles into Practice Cards*. Accessed 12th May 2019 webarchive.nationalarchives.gov.uk/20130401151715/../DCSF-00012-2007.pdf

DCSF. (2008) *Every Child a Talker:Guidance for Early Language Lead Practitioners*. Nottingham: DCSF Publications.

DCSF. (2009) *Learning, Playing and Interacting: Good Practice in the Early Years Foundation Stage*. Nottingham: DCSF Publications.

DCSF. (2010) *Social and Emotional Aspects of Development: Guidance for Practitioners Working in the Early Years Foundation Stage*. Nottingham: DCSF Publications.

Dewey, J. (1938) *Experience and Education*. New York: Collier Books.

DfE. (2018) *Early Years Foundation Stage: Setting the Standards for Learning, Development and Care for Children from Birth to Five*. Nottingham: DfE.

Dweke, C. (1999) *Self Theories: Their Role in the Motivation, Personality, and Development*. Philadelphia, PA: Psychology Press.

Dweke, S. (2015) Growth. *British Journal of Educational Psychology*. 85(2), 242–245.

Elfer, P., Goldschmied, E. and Selleck, D. (2003) *Key Persons in the Nursery, Building Relationships for Quality Provision*. London: David Fulton.

Field, F. (2010) *The Foundation Years: Preventing Poor Children Becoming Poor Adults*. London: Cabinet Office.

Forbes, R. (2004) *Beginning to Play*. London: Open University Press.

Gibbs, G. (1988) *Learning by Doing: A Guide to Teaching and Learning Methods*. London: FEU.

Greenland, P. (2000) *Hopping Home Backwards: Body Intelligence and Movement Play*. Leeds: Jabadao Publication.

Goldschmied, E. and Jackson, S. (1994) *People under Three: Young Children in Day Care*. London and New York: Routledge.

Hannaford, C. (2005) *Smart Moves: Why Learning Is Not All in Your Head*. 2nd ed. Utah: Great River Books.

Hughes, A. (2016) *Developing Play for the under 3's – The Treasure Basket and Heuristic Play*. Oxon: Routledge.

Janzen, M.D. (2008) Where Is the (Postmodern) Child in Early Childhood Education Research? *Early Years an International Journal of Research and Development*. 28(3), 287–297.

Kolb, D. (1984) *Experiential Learning Experience as a Source of Learning and Development*. New Jersey: Prentice Hall.

Laevers, F. (1994) *Defining and Assessing Quality in Early Childhood Education*. Belgium: Laevers University Press.

Laevers, F., Vandenbussche, E., Kog, M. and Depondt, L. (1997) *A Process-Orientated Child Monitoring System for Young Children*. Experiential Education Series, No 2. Centre for Eperiential Education.

Macleod-Brunell. (2004) *Advanced Early Years Care and Education for Levels 4 and 5*. Oxford: Heinemen Education.

Manning-Morton, J. and Thorpe, M. (2015) *Two-year-Olds in Early Years Settings: Journeys of Discovery*. Berkshire: Open University Press.

Moon, J. (2004) *A Handbook of Reflective and Experiential Learning: Theory and Practice*. London: Routledge.

National Literacy Trust. (2018) *Making the Most of the Home Learning Environment*. Accessed 12th May 2019 https://literacytrust.org.uk/resources/making-most-home-learning-environment/

NHS. (2019) *Overview Postnatal Depression*. Accessed 12th April 2019 www.nhs.uk/conditions/post-natal-depression/

Nutbrown, C. (2011) *Threads of Thinking: Schemas and Young Children's Learning*. 4th ed. London: Sage.

Nutbrown, C. (2012) *Foundations for Quality: The Independent Review of Early Education and Childcare Qualifications Final Report*. Cheshire: DfE.

Pollard, A. (ed) (2014) *Reflective Teaching in Schools*. London: Bloomsbury.

Penderi, E. and Petrogiannis, K. (2011) Parental Ethontheories and Customs of Child-rearing in Two Roma Urban Communities in Greece: Examining the Developmental Niche of the 6 Year Old Child. *Journal of Social, Evolutioary, and Cultural Psychology*. 5(1), 32–50.

Robinson, T. (2007) *TED Talk Do Schools Kill Creativity?* Accessed 10th May 2019 www.ted.com/talks/ken_robinson_says_schools_kill_creativity?language=en

Schon, D. (1983) *Educating the Reflective Practitioner*. San Francisco, CA: Jossey-Bass.

Stewart, N. (2011) *How Children Learn. The Characteristics of Effective Early Learning*. London: The British Association for Early Childhood.

Tickell, C. (2011) *The Early Years: Foundations for Life, Health and Learning: An Independent Report on the Early Years Foundation Stage to Her Majesty's Government*. London: DfE.

Travarthen, C. and Aitken, K.J. (1994) Brain Development, Infant Communication and Empathy Disorders: Intrinsic Factors in Child Mental Health. *Development and Psychopathology*. 6(4), 597–633.

Further reading

Brock, A. (2015) *The Early Years Reflective Practice Handbook*. Oxon: Routledge.
Every Child a Talker (Ecat) – The National Archives

References

Field, F. (2010) *The Foundation Years: Preventing Poor Children Becoming Poor Adults*. London: Cabinet Office.

Goddard Blyth, S. (2005) *The Well Balanced Child; Movement and Early Learning*. 2nd ed. Gloucestershire: Hawthorn Press.

Goddard Blyth, S. (2018) *Movement Your Child's First Language*. Gloucestershire: Hawthorn Press.

Maude, P. (2001) *Physical Children, Active Teaching: Investigating Physical Literacy*. Buckingham: Open University Press.

Moon, J. (2004) *A Handbook of Reflective and Experiential Learning: Theory and Practice*. London: Routledge.

Websites

www.bbc.co.uk – CBBC – Growth Mindsets: helping your child try new things
www.bbc.co.uk/cbeebies/grownups/help-your-child-try-new-things
www.gettingsmart.com
www.naeyc.org – NAEYC: *Learning stories*:
www.naeyc.org/resources/pubs/tyc/dec2015/learning-stories
www.ncb.org.uk – Parents, Early years and Learning (PEAL)
www.ican.org.uk
www.literacytrust.org.uk

Index

Abbott, L. 52
adult role 97, 99, 102
Ainsworth, M. 22
Aitken, K.J. 54
assessment 137–139, 145
Atherton, F. 141
Athey, C. 110, 116
attachment theory 21–23, 82; behaviours 24; factors affecting 27–28

behaviour 24, 30; emotions 30–32, 86; impulsive 30; tantrums 90
biting 87–88
Blehar, M. 22
Boud, D. 10, 138
Bowlby, J. 22
brain development 30, 35–36, 42, 45
Brierley, J. 11, 103, 115, 123
Bronfenbrenner, E. 63
Bruce, T. 101–102
building attachments 83–85

Carr, M. 73
cephalo- caudal development 38
characteristics of effective play 99–107
Claxton, G. 73
cognitive development 97, 109; learning 70; skills 33
collaborative relationships 60
communication 45–56; language development 50; spoken language 47–50
confidence 8, 12, 21, 70–71, 79, 97, 99, 131
containing schema 113, 117, 128, 129–131
creativity 71, 104–106, 145
critical reflection 7, 8–10, 12
Csikszentmihalyi, M. 103
culture 62–66
curriculum 137, 145

Department for Children, Schools and Families (DCSF) 27, 47, 48, 101
Department for Education (DfE) 79
Dewey, J. 13
dispositions 29, 67, 69–77
documentation 137; pedagogical 138–139; process 142
Dweke, C. 74, 75, 76

early language 47, 67
echolalia 53
Elfer, P. 80, 83, 92
emotions 1, 18; development 21–30; regulation 31, 36; resilience 24
empathy 60
Enclosing schema 113, 133
english as additional language 48, 55
environment for learning 95–107, 123–135
Every Child a Talker 48

family 80, 88–89; life 59, 62; culture 63
Field, F. 35
fine motor 41
Forbes, R. 46
friendship 29–30
frustration 31–32

gender 29
Gibbs, G. 16–18, 32
Golschmied, E. 118
graphical representation 115–116
Greenland, J. 35, 38
gross motor skills 34, 41

hand preference 39
Hannaford, C. 35–37, 38, 42
hearing difficulties 55
heuristic play 118–119
home learning environment 64, 66–68

Index

Hughes, A. 135
hunger 31

imagination 104, 105
incidental observations 144
involvement scales 140–141

Janzen, M.D. 105

Keogh, R. 10, 138
key person 23, 32, 79–93; relationships 25, 82 – 84; role 79–81
kinaesthetic 42, 125
Kolb, D. 17, 18, 52, 56

Laevers, F. 103, 141
Langston, A. 52
language 120, 132; development 45–55; spoken 105, 141; use of 130
learning stories 145
learnt response tantrums 31
listening 46, 49, 54–55

Macleod-Brunell 15
macrosytems 64
Malaguzzi, L. 145
Manning-Morton, J. 31
mesosytem 64
microsystems 64
mindset 69–77
Moon, J. 10, 15
motivation 69, 103–104, 110
movement 37

nappies 47, 85, 89–90
National Literacy Trust 52
NHS 28
Nutbrown, C. 59, 65, 115, 117

observation focused 141; incidental 144; participant 143; planned 141
outdoor environment 14, 36, 101, 123, 128–130

palmar grasp 39
Parental involvement 59–61; relationships 60; styles 61–62
pedagogical documentation 138–139, 145
pedagogy 97–98

Penderi, E. 63
Petrogiannis, K. 63
physical development 33–44
pincer movement 40
play choices 25; space 132–133
Pollard, A. 14
proprioceptors 41–42
proximodistal development 38–39
proximity 80, 84–85

reflection 5, 7–9, 14–16; critical 10; formal 10, 12; informal 10
resilience 24, 37, 69, 74, 103, 131
risk assessment 43, 126
risky play 43
Robinson, T. 105
rotation schema 134
routines 92–93, 104, 144

schema 109–121
Schon, D. 14
self confidence 24, 28, 29, 67
self esteem 28, 29, 37, 62, 67, 139
sensory stimulus 42
separation anxiety 25–27, 82–86
settling in 25, 81–86, 139
sleep 31, 90, 91
stammering 53, 54
Stewart, N. 70
stuttering 53, 54

tantrums 31, 32, 90
Thorpe, M. 31
Tickell, C. 99, 100
tiredness 31, 90
toilet training 89–90
trajectory schema 116, 117, 128, 129, 132
transporting schema 114, 116, 126, 127 134
Travarthen, C. 54

values 9, 92, 145
vestibular system 42

Walker, D. 10, 138
Wall, S. 22
Waters, E. 22
Wendy, L. 73
working with parents 60